THE WISDOM OF THE WORD
LOVE

Also by
Rhinold Ponder
and Michele Tuck-Ponder

THE WISDOM OF THE WORD

FAITH

THE WISDOM OF THE WORD
LOVE

Great African-American Sermons

EDITED BY

Rhinold Ponder and Michele Tuck-Ponder

FOREWORD BY

Dr. Gardner C. Taylor

ILLUSTRATIONS BY

Bruce Waldman

CROWN PUBLISHERS, INC.
NEW YORK

Grateful acknowledgment is made to the following for permission to reprint previously published material:
"A Christmas Sermon on Peace" by Dr. Martin Luther King, Jr. Copyright © 1967 by Martin Luther King, Jr. Copyright renewed 1995 by Coretta Scott King. Reprinted by permission of the heirs to Estate of Martin Luther King, Jr., c/o Writer's House Inc., as agent for the proprietor. "Where Is the Love" by Floyd H. Flake. Reprinted by permission of the author. "A New Commandment" by Jeremiah A. Wright, Jr. Reprinted by permission of the author. "Liberating Love" by Toinette M. Eugene from *And Blessed Is She*, edited by David A. Farmer and Edwina Hunter. Copyright © 1990 by David A. Farmer and Edwina Hunter. Reprinted by permission of HarperCollins Publishers, Inc. "How Much Do You Love Jesus?" by Reginald T. Jackson. Reprinted by permission of the author. "True Love" by Felicia Yvonne Thomas. Reprinted by permission of the author. "From Paternalism to Partnership" by John Richard Foulkes, Sr. from *Out of Mighty Waters* (St. Louis, Chalice Press, 1994). Reprinted by permission of Chalice Press. "A Mother at the Cross" by C. L. Franklin from *Give Me This Mountain*. Reprinted by permission of the University of Illinois Press and the estate of the author. "Love of Self" by Howard Thurman from the sermon series *Growing in Love*, by Howard Thurman. Copyright © Howard Thurman.

PUBLISHED BY CROWN PUBLISHERS, INC.,
201 East 50th Street, New York, New York 10022.

Member of the Crown Publishing Group.

Random House, Inc. New York, Toronto, London, Sydney, Auckland

http://www.randomhouse.com/

CROWN is a trademark of Crown Publishers, Inc.

Printed in the United States of America

Design by Julie Duquet

Library of Congress Cataloging-in-Publication Data

The wisdom of the Word: love/edited by Rhinold Ponder and Michele Tuck-Ponder—1st ed.
        p.   cm.
1. Love—Religious aspects—Christianity—Sermons.   2. Sermons, American—Afro-American authors.   I. Ponder, Rhinold.   II. Tuck, Michele.
                        BV4639.W55   1997
252'.0089'96073—dc20   96-27368
                        CIP

ISBN 0-517-70592-3

10   9   8   7   6   5   4   3   2   1

First Edition

Contents

ACKNOWLEDGMENTS

In this second volume of *Wisdom of the Word*, we happily repeat our gratitude and appreciation to those who have made the success of this exciting project possible.

We would like to express our deepest gratitude to Rev. Reginald T. Jackson, pastor of St. Matthew's A.M.E. Church in Orange, New Jersey; Professor Peter Paris of Princeton Theological Seminary; Dr. Jeremiah A. Wright, Jr., pastor of Trinity United Church of Christ in Chicago; Dr. Cleo LaRue of the New Brunswick Theological Seminary; and Dr. Gerald Davis. Their efforts in identifying some of America's greatest messengers of the Word and their advice on evaluating these works were invaluable.

Additionally, we thank Dr. Samuel D. Proctor and Dr. Gardner C. Taylor, for gracing and inaugurating the first two volumes of this series with the wisdom of their insight, experience, and love.

We offer special thanks to Rosalyn Andrews, Rev. Warren Dennis, Charles Hardaway, Adrienne Ingrum, Dr. Calvin Morris, and Minnie Wright of the Interdenominational Theological Center in Atlanta, and to Dr. Dolly McPherson, Dr. Alvin Ponder, III, Dr. Russell Adams, and Bishop Prince Taylor. Each of them played a special and essential role in shaping this project.

We extend a special acknowledgment to our staff—Angelique Harris, Sharahn Thomas, and Ava Gascer—for their dedication and hard work.

Great thanks and blessings to Carol Taylor, our editor, who had the insight and foresight to see the need for this historical and spiritual undertaking.

And as always, we offer our love and eternal gratitude to our parents, Carrie B. Ponder and William A. Tuck, who have loved us and prepared us for the possibilities of our own good.

And most important, we thank God, who makes all things possible.

Foreword

by

Dr. Gardner C. Taylor

L OVE AND FAITH are the spiritual muscles of life. Just as your body is composed of physical muscles—without which it cannot function—without love and faith, the spirit cannot thrive. Faith and love are basic to our existence, the way we look at things, the way we treat people, and the way we conduct our lives. The love of God in us produces faith in Him. And that faith in God gives us the confidence to know that things will work out for the best when we work together for the love of the Lord.

Today the virtual disappearance of the "love ethic" has had its effect on us all. Our society has become loaded with hate and faithlessness. There has begun to be a circling of the wagons, a callousness in our society to an extent I have never seen—from people behind counters to radio airwaves, to within the home. I don't know anything needed in this country as much as practice of the idea of love—not an erotic kind of love, but an outgoing goodwill; for which the word "agape" stood in the New Testament. Our society is in shorter supply of goodwill than almost anything else.

We have allowed the institutions of society to become hardened and impersonal. This is having a serious effect on society in general. We no longer talk in civil tones. Everything is an insult, a put-down. We have made a commitment to greed, and our society is deteriorating because of it. The people responsible for opinion setting—schools, churches, public-communication media—need to begin looking at how frayed the fabric of our society has become, and should begin to discuss the need for goodwill.

We must begin by looking at how we treat other people. In our personal relations, a sense of regard for the value of every other individual will do a great deal to change the way we treat them. I do not think there is any basis for a "love ethic" that does not largely take into account the preciousness, the importance of the individual. The New Testament gives a sense of one's worth. Christ thought every person was worth dying for; that is the basis of our preciousness.

As African Americans, we need to cultivate among ourselves — in our churches and in our schools—the idea that anger is not an answer; it is self-defeating. When energy is spent on hatred and resentment, it is used up needlessly. Jesus said, "Do unto others as you would have them do unto you." Somehow that simple notion has been lost.

Those times when the plight of blacks in America has been at the forefront of the nation's thinking, have also been the times when the nation has thought seriously and deeply of goodwill and love. It may well be that a nation's sense of goodwill is brought about by the presence of a minority community. And it also stands to reason that the "love ethic" manifests itself mostly in the presence of need within and without.

This volume of The Wisdom of the Word is sensitive to human need. These sermons point to human life under the pressure and light of God's presence; that is the only way that life can be fully lived. These words help us to see God's presence and to create a loving atmosphere. In that sense they have extraordinary value. I encourage the reader to consider these sermons as an exercise in the development of spiritual muscles — helping us to grow stronger in our love and faith in God and each other.

INTRODUCTION

There are three things that
remain —faith, hope, and love —and
the greatest of these is love.
1 CORINTHIANS 13:13

W*isdom of the Word: Love* is propelled by the greatest love of all — God's love in giving us Jesus Christ, who died for our sins so that we might experience eternal life. The story of Jesus' life, death, and resurrection is known throughout the world by churchgoers and unchurched alike. However, it is one thing to be familiar with the story of Christ; it is quite another to engage, absorb, and spread God's love. God's servants and messengers of African-American descent have been dedicated to spreading God's love through preaching and service ever since enslaved Africans "corrected" the self-serving biblical interpretations of their oppressors.

Historically, it is love, as illustrated by the life and resurrection of Christ, which has sustained the African-American community through centuries of servitude, segregation, economic enslavement, and racism. As a community, African Americans have long identified with the example of Christ as He responded to oppression, castigation, imprisonment, and injustice with faith, hope, and love. Love, as the base value of all decision making, has been our community's most powerful, effective, and regenerative response to the challenging aspects of our condition.

Of equal significance, however, is the impact that our love has had on the world. Love is infectious; it is a force multiplier. African Americans, often led by great religious leaders and people with strong spiritual values, have on many occasions been the conscience of the nation. Without the strength born of love, there would be neither "emancipation," "economic empowerment," nor "civil rights." God's servants within this volume, including Howard Thurman, Dr. Martin Luther King, Jr., and Dr. Jeremiah A. Wright, to name a very few, were among the great African-American messengers to inject the "love dialogue" into our recent political-cultural history.

Yet, now we are probably faced with our most challenging times in God's service. Just as love has sustained the African-American community and has enhanced our nation, the absence of love signals and contributes to our nation's deterioration. Drugs, violence, and corrupted values have cast themselves over America like pestilence from the Old Testament. Our civility has diminished; our politics have been poisoned with hate, thinly disguised as pragmatism, our spirits are constantly bombarded by violent and selfish self-images. Perhaps worst, we have collectively lowered our standards for human interaction. We now measure our commitment to mankind in units of tolerance, not love and compassion. This is our challenge as a nation and as a member of the worldwide "sister- and brotherhood."

Chosen for their clarity, relevance, and ability to bring life to the Word, the wonderful sermons within this volume are merely a sample of the great work of African-American messengers who have engaged the challenge. For example, in his sermon, Dr. Martin Luther King, Jr., accurately conveys the sense of dread, despair, cruelty, and cynicism which pervade our daily existence. The message here is clear and real: Our present condition is unacceptable and reversible. Love—our embrace of God's love and our commitment to resurrecting that love through our own lives—is the cure to our condition.

The sermons herein also address different aspects of and types of love. For example, the preeminence of Howard Thurman still graces us years after his death as he compels us to consider self-love in light of God's power. In one of his most memorable sermons, C. L. Franklin extols maternal love. And in "How Much Do You Love Jesus?" Reginald T. Jackson forces us to address our love for the material world versus our love of God.

In addition to describing and extolling love, these sermons instruct us on how to maintain, express, and utilize love. This is exemplified in the sermons of master preachers such as Dr. Jeremiah A. Wright, Jr., who advises us that love is hard work, so hard that Jesus knew it was worth dying for. And Toinette M. Eugene tells us that God's love liberates us if we heed the command to exalt it and pass it on.

So, we offer *Wisdom of the Word: Love* to you as a gift of hope and a challenge for engagement, as a reflection of African-American cultural tradition and a promise of personal transformation; as a spiritual road map; and as an exaltation of God's greatest gift to us all. We pray that you prosper as you accept the challenge.

Love is very patient and kind, never jealous or envious, never boastful or proud, never haughty or selfish or rude. Love does not demand its own way. It is not irritable or touchy. It does not hold grudges and will hardly even notice when others do it wrong. It is never glad about injustice, but rejoices whenever truth wins out. If you love someone you will be loyal to him no matter what the cost. You will always believe in him, always expect the best of him, and always stand your ground in defending him.

1 CORINTHIANS 13:4–7

A Christmas Sermon
on Peace
Rev. Dr. Martin Luther King, Jr.

*In this eloquent sermon, we are called to consider our
struggle for world peace through love, nonviolence, and an
understanding of humanity's interrelatedness across racial,
ethnic, tribal, and economic divisions.*

PEACE ON EARTH ...
This Christmas season finds us a rather bewildered human race. We have neither peace within nor peace without. Everywhere paralyzing fears harrow people by day and haunt them by night. Our world is sick with war; everywhere we turn we see its ominous possibilities. And yet, my friends, the Christmas hope for peace and good will toward all men can no longer be dismissed as a kind of pious dream of some utopian. If we don't have good will toward men in this world, we will destroy ourselves by the misuse of our own instruments and our own power. Wisdom born of experience should tell us that war is obsolete. There may have been a time when war served as a negative good by preventing the spread and growth of an evil force, but the very destructive power of modern weapons of warfare eliminates even the possibility that war may any longer serve as a negative good. And so, if we assume that life is worth living, if we assume that mankind has a right to survive, then we must find an alternative to war—and so let us this morning explore the conditions for peace. Let us this morning think anew on the meaning of that Christmas hope: "Peace on Earth, Good Will toward Men." And as we explore these conditions, I would like to suggest that modern man really go all out to study the meaning of nonviolence, its philosophy and its strategy.

We have experimented with the meaning of nonviolence in our struggle for racial justice in the United States, but now the time has come for man to experiment with nonviolence in all areas of human conflict, and that means nonviolence on an international scale.

Now let me suggest first that if we are to have peace on earth, our loyalties must become ecumenical rather than sectional. Our loyalties must transcend our race, our tribe, our class, and our nation; and this means we must develop a world perspective. No individual can live alone; no nation can live alone, and as long as we try, the more we are going to have war in this world. Now the judgment of God is upon us, and we must either learn to live together as brothers or we are all going to perish together as fools.

Yes, as nations and individuals, we are interdependent. I have spoken to you before of our visit to India some years ago. It was a marvelous experience; but I say to you this morning that there were those depressing moments. How can one avoid being depressed when one sees with one's own eyes evidences of millions of people going to bed hungry at night? How can one avoid being depressed when one sees with one's own eyes thousands of people sleeping on the sidewalks at night? More than a million people sleep on the sidewalks of Bombay every night, more than half a million sleep on the sidewalks of Calcutta every night. They have no houses to go into. They have no beds to sleep in. As I beheld these conditions, something within me cried out: "Can we in America stand idly by and not be concerned?" And an answer came: "Oh, no!" And I started thinking about the fact that right here in our country we spend millions of dollars every day to store surplus food; and I said to myself "I know where we can store that food free of charge—in the wrinkled stomachs of the millions of God's children in Asia, Africa, Latin America, and even in our own nation, who go to bed hungry at night."

It really boils down to this: that all life is interrelated. We are all caught in an inescapable network of mutuality, tied into a single garment of destiny. Whatever affects one directly, affects all indirectly. We are made to live together because of the interrelated structure of reality. Did you ever stop to think that you can't leave for your job in the morning without being dependent on most of the world? You get up in the morning and go to the bathroom and reach over for the sponge, and that's handed to you by a Pacific Islander. You reach for a bar of soap, and that's given to you at the hands of a Frenchman. And then you go into the kitchen to drink your coffee for the morning, and that's poured into your cup by a South American. And maybe you want tea: That's poured into your cup by a Chinese. Or maybe you're desirous of having cocoa for breakfast, and that's poured into your cup by a West African. And then you reach over for your toast, and that's given to you at the hands of an English-speaking farmer, not to mention the baker. And before you finish eating breakfast in the morning, you've depended on more than half of the world. This is the way our universe is structured, this is its interrelated quality. We aren't going to have peace on earth until we recognize this basic fact of the interrelated structure of all reality.

Now let me say, secondly, that if we are to have peace in the world, men and nations must embrace the nonviolent affirmation that ends and means must cohere. One of the great philosophical debates of history has been over the whole question of means and ends. And there have always been those who argued that the end justifies the means, that the means really aren't important. The important thing is to get to the end, you see.

So, if you're seeking to develop a just society, they say, the important thing is to get there, and the means are really unimportant; any means will do so long as they get you there — they may be violent, they may be untruthful means; they may even be unjust means to a just end. There have been those who have argued this throughout history. But we will never have peace in the world until men everywhere recognize that ends are not cut off from means, because the means represent the ideal in the making, and the end in process, and ultimately you can't reach good ends through evil means, because the means represent the seed and the end represents the tree.

It's one of the strangest things that all the great military geniuses of the world have talked about peace. The conquerors of old who came killing in pursuit of peace — Alexander, Julius Caesar, Charlemagne, and Napoleon — were akin in seeking a peaceful world order. If you will read *Mein Kampf* closely enough, you will discover that Hitler contended that everything he did in Germany was for peace. And the leaders of the world today talk eloquently about peace. Every time we drop our bombs in North Vietnam,

President Johnson talks eloquently about peace. What is the problem? They are talking about peace as a distant goal, as an end we seek, but one day we must come to see that peace is not merely a distant goal we seek, but that it is a means by which we arrive at that goal. We must pursue peaceful ends through peaceful means. All of this is saying that, in the final analysis, means and ends must cohere because the end is preexistent in the means, and ultimately destructive means cannot bring about constructive ends.

Now let me say that the next thing we must be concerned about if we are to have peace on earth and good will toward men is the nonviolent affirmation of the sacredness of all human life. Every man is somebody because he is a child of God. And so when we say, "Thou shalt not kill," we're really saying that human life is too sacred to be taken on the battlefields of the world. Man is more than a tiny vagary of whirling electrons or a wisp of smoke from a limitless smoldering. Man is a child of God, made in His image, and therefore must be respected as such. Until men see this everywhere, until nations see this everywhere, we will be fighting wars. One day somebody should remind us that, even though there may be political and ideological differences between us, the Vietnamese are our brothers, the Russians are our brothers, the Chinese are our brothers; and one day we've got to sit down together at the table of brotherhood. But in Christ there is neither Jew nor Gentile. In Christ there is neither male nor female. In Christ there is neither Communist nor capitalist. In Christ, somehow, there is neither bound nor free. We are all one in Christ Jesus. And when we truly believe in the sacredness of human personality, we won't exploit people, we won't trample over people with the iron feet of oppression, we won't kill anybody.

There are three words for "love" in the Greek New Testament; one is the word "eros." Eros is a sort of esthetic, romantic love. Plato used to talk about it a great deal in his dialogues, the yearning of the soul for the realm of the divine. And there is and can always be something beautiful about eros, even in its expressions of romance. Some of the most beautiful love in all of the world has been expressed this way.

Then the Greek language talks about "philia," which is another

word for love, and philia is a kind of intimate love between personal friends. This is the kind of love you have for those people
that you get along with well, and those whom you like on this level
you love because you are loved.

Then the Greek language has another word for love, and that is
the word "agape." Agape is more than romantic love, it is more
than friendship. Agape is understanding, creative, redemptive
good will toward all men. Agape is an overflowing love which
seeks nothing in return. Theologians would say that it is the love
of God operating in the human heart. When you rise to love on
this level, you love all men not because you like them, not because
their ways appeal to you, but you love them because God loves
them. This is what Jesus meant when he said, "Love your enemies." And I'm happy that he didn't say, "Like your enemies," because there are some people that I find it pretty difficult to like.
Liking is an affectionate emotion, and I can't like anybody who
would bomb my home. I can't like anybody who would exploit me.
I can't like anybody who would trample over me with injustices. I
can't like them. I can't like anybody who threatens to kill me day
in and day out. But Jesus reminds us that love is greater than liking. Love is understanding, creative, redemptive good will toward
all men. And I think this is where we are, as a people, in our struggle for racial justice. We can't ever give up. We must work passionately and unrelentingly for first-class citizenship. We must
never let up in our determination to remove every vestige of segregation and discrimination from our nation, but we shall not in the
process relinquish our privilege to love.

I've seen too much hate to want to hate, myself, and I've seen
hate on the faces of too many sheriffs, too many white citizens'
councilors, and too many Klansmen of the South to want to hate,
myself; and every time I see it, I say to myself, hate is too great a
burden to bear. Somehow we must be able to stand up before our
most bitter opponents and say: "We shall match your capacity to
inflict suffering by our capacity to endure suffering. We will meet
your physical force with soul force. Do to us what you will and we
will still love you. We cannot in all good conscience obey your unjust laws and abide by the unjust system, because noncooperation

with evil is as much a moral obligation as is cooperation with good, and so throw us in jail and we will still love you. Bomb our homes and threaten our children, and, as difficult as it is, we will still love you. Send your hooded perpetrators of violence into our communities at the midnight hour and drag us out on some wayside road and leave us half-dead as you beat us, and we will still love you. Send your propaganda agents around the country, and make it appear that we are not fit, culturally and otherwise, for integration, and we'll still love you. But be assured that we'll wear you down by our capacity to suffer, and one day we will win our freedom. We will not only win freedom for ourselves; we will so appeal to your heart and conscience that we will win you in the process, and our victory will be a double victory."

If there is to be peace on earth and good will toward men, we must finally believe in the ultimate morality of the universe, and believe that all reality hinges on moral foundations. Something must remind us of this as we once again stand in the Christmas season and think of the Easter season simultaneously, for the two somehow go together. Christ came to show us the way. Men love darkness rather than the light, and they crucified him, and there on Good Friday on the cross it was still dark, but then Easter came, and Easter is an eternal reminder of the fact that the truth-crushed earth will rise again. Easter justifies Carlyle in saying, "No lie can live forever." And so this is our faith, as we continue to hope for peace on earth and good will toward men: Let us know that in the process we have cosmic companionship.

In 1963, on a sweltering August afternoon, we stood in Washington, D.C., and talked to the nation about many things. Toward the end of that afternoon, I tried to talk to the nation about a dream that I had, and I must confess to you today that not long after talking about that dream I started seeing it turn into a nightmare. I remember the first time I saw that dream turn into a nightmare, just a few weeks after I had talked about it. It was when four beautiful, unoffending, innocent Negro girls were murdered in a church in Birmingham, Alabama. I watched that dream turn into a nightmare as I moved through the ghettos of the nation and saw my black brothers and sisters perishing on a lonely island of poverty in the midst of a vast ocean of material prosperity, and saw the nation doing nothing to grapple with the Negroes' problem of poverty. I saw that dream turn into a nightmare as I watched my black brothers and sisters in the midst of anger and understandable outrage, in the midst of their hurt, in the midst of their disappointment, turn to misguided riots to try to solve that problem. I saw that dream turn into a nightmare as I watched the war in Vietnam escalating, and as I saw so-called military advisors, sixteen thousand strong, turn into fighting soldiers until today over five hundred thousand American boys are fighting on Asian soil. Yes, I am personally the victim of deferred dreams, of blasted hopes, but in spite of that I close today by saying I still have a dream, because, you know, you can't give up in life. If you lose hope, somehow you lose that vitality that keeps life moving, you lose that courage to be, that quality that helps you go on in spite of all. And so today I still have a dream.

I have a dream that one day men will rise up and come to see that they are made to live together as brothers. I still have a dream this morning that one day every Negro in this country, every colored person in the world, will be judged on the basis of the content of his character rather than the color of his skin, and every man will respect the dignity and worth of human personality. I still have a dream that one day the idle industries of Appalachia will be revitalized, and the empty stomachs of Mississippi will be filled, and brotherhood will be more than a few words at the end of a prayer, but rather the first order of business on every legislative agenda. I still have a dream today that one day justice will roll down like water, and righteousness like a mighty stream. I still have a dream today that in all of our statehouses and city halls men will be elected to go there who will do justly and love mercy and walk humbly with their God. I still have a dream today that one day war will come to an end, that men will beat their swords into plowshares and their spears into pruning hooks, that nations will no longer rise up against nations, neither will they study war any more. I still have a dream today that one day the lamb and the lion will lie down together and every man will sit under his own vine and fig tree and none shall be afraid. I still have a dream today that one day every valley shall be exalted and every mountain and hill will be made low, the rough places will be made smooth and the crooked places straight, and the glory of the Lord shall be revealed, and all flesh shall see it together. I still have a dream that with this faith we will be able to adjourn the councils of despair and bring new light into the dark chambers of pessimism. With this faith we will be able to speed up the day when there will be peace on earth and good will toward men. It will be a glorious day; the morning stars will sing together, and the sons of God will shout for joy.

WHERE IS THE LOVE?
Floyd H. Flake

The life and teachings of Jesus present to us a challenge to examine the dichotomy between the practical and rhetorical expression of the principle of love to all humanity.

LUKE 10:25–37

"And, behold, a certain lawyer stood up, and tempted him, saying, Master, what shall I do to inherit eternal life? He said unto him, *What is written in the law? How readest thou?* And he answering said, Thou shalt love the Lord thy God with all thy heart, and with all thy soul, and with all thy strength, and with all thy mind; and thy neighbor as thyself. And he said unto him, *Thou hast answered right: this do, and thou shalt live.* But he, willing to justify himself, said unto Jesus, And who is my neighbor? And Jesus answering said, *A certain man went down from Jerusalem to Jericho, and fell among thieves, which stripped him of his raiment, and wounded him, and departed, leaving him half dead. And by chance there came down a certain priest that way: and when he saw him, he passed by on the other side. And likewise a Levite, when he was at the place, came and looked on him, and passed by on the other side. But a certain Samaritan, as he journeyed, came where he was: and when he saw him, he had compassion on him, and went to him, and bound up his wounds, pouring in oil and wine, and set him on his own beast, and brought him to an inn, and took care of him. And on the morrow when he departed, he took out two pence, and gave them to the host, and said unto him, Take care of him; and whatsoever thou spendest more, when I come again, I will repay thee. Which now of these three, thinkest thou, was neighbor unto him that fell among the thieves?* And he said, He that showed mercy on him. Then said Jesus unto him, Go, and do thou likewise."

ALMOST ON A daily basis we are faced with the reality that there exists in our society a dichotomy between what we preach and teach about love and the practical application of the principle of love when we are faced with opportunities to put it into practice. Most pastors have historically preached on themes that command the people of God to love God and express it through their response to the needs of others. This theme is compatible with the teachings of the Decalogue and is timeless in its intent for all people who are followers of God and profess a belief in the Christian virtues of the faith. No virtue carries more weight than love. Colossians 3:14 records *"Faith, hope and love, and above all these things put on love, which is the bond of perfectness."* In spite of the emphasis that is placed on the virtue of love, there is much evidence that our relationship to, and practice of love, is more often rhetorical than real. What the world needs now is real love.

Our practice of the virtues of love rarely reaches the level of our verbiage about them. The evidence is all around us and is seen in the faces of those in our society who suffer. They need love, but never really come to know love because it is not forthcoming from the people that they expect to show them their love. Instead, they often show a callous insensitivity to their plight, their suffering, and their pitiful condition. It is heard in the voices of talk-show hosts, who demean those who have suffered some misfortune. Even the agenda of the Christian Coalition is void of an understanding of the Lord's teaching on love.

If the embodiment of Christianity is centered in the theme of love, as expressed by God having given the world its best gift in the person of Jesus Christ, then one must ask some serious questions regarding the role of the church in a changing society. How can the Christian church and Christian people turn their faces to the myriad problems of homelessness, poverty, family disintegration, racism, and gender assaults on women? How can the church of Jesus Christ, who is the embodiment of love, lack concern for AIDS victims, and turn its eyes away from the many children who suffer malnutrition because of a lack of food in a nation of wealth? How can we justify paying CEOs of Fortune 500 companies millions of dollars to downsize, while at the same time reducing the number of jobs available to those who need them the most? The wealth of this nation is juxtaposed to the conditions that have become so prevalent in most of our urban and rural communities, where people have been left to suffer because jobs have been exported to countries where labor is cheap, and no replacement industries have been found for the individuals who have been left behind. The problem has been exacerbated by political attacks on the basic programs that have provided meager hope in the midst of otherwise hopeless situations.

Attempts to make draconian changes in welfare, exorbitant cuts in education, proposed block granting of Medicare and Medicaid, elimination of the Earned Income Tax Credit for the poor, and reduction of scholarships has made it difficult for persons who have depended on these entitlements for their survival. Do we dare to believe that our proclamation of love is truly operative in this world when compassion and sensitivity seem to have lost their way to the hearts of those who are the power brokers and decision makers in America and the world? It is a shame that we have lost our ability to love those who are considered to be the least: the poor, the uneducated, and the infirm. That is the reason they killed Jesus. He was reversing the order of things, creating more openings and opportunities for the poor and oppressed. But, more than that, by loving them and teaching them to love one another, their hopes for the future were brighter than their past. His love touched their hearts in ways that inspired them to accept His transforming grace for themselves, and respond in love by sharing the benefits of their grace to meet the needs of other people.

Luke 10:25 introduces a parable that speaks to Christ's concern about the love that must be expressed by all humanity, both to

God and to the other human beings who share this planet with us regardless of their status or condition in life. In this text, a lawyer, who in Jewish culture was a professional teacher, an expert versed in the Mosaic law, and a man of great influence and importance, stood up in one of Jesus' teaching sessions to ask a question. It was a hard and comprehensive question that attracted the attention of Jesus and those who were seated and listening to His teachings. It was a tricky question intended to embarrass Jesus. It was presented as a test of Jesus' skill at answering questions of the laws which guided daily life in Israel. He asked Jesus, "What must I do to inherit eternal life?" Jesus answered by posing two questions to him, "What is written in the law? And, How do you read it?" Jesus' frame of reference is the pivotal text of Deuteronomy 6:5: *"Love the Lord your God with all of your heart and with all of your soul and with all your strength."* The lawyer, like many of us, no doubt believed himself to be in conformity with the law and probably felt some relief in knowing that he had no difficulty answering the question. In his mind, he had been faithful in his duty toward God. He was doubtlessly at ease with himself knowing that he had scrupulously paid his tithes, rigidly observed all of the mandated feasts, was obedient to the laws of fasting, and did not neglect his prayers.

If our love of God was merely defined in terms of responses to ritual, form, fashion, tradition, and obedience to law, then the lawyer would have been able to continue to be at ease knowing that he had indeed fulfilled all of his responsibilities to God. However, the second part of the law presents an even greater challenge for him and for us. It commands us, as an expression of one's love for God to "Love your neighbor as you love yourself." The lawyer, like many of us, was caught off guard. He could not respond directly to the question, even though he had professed a knowledge and belief and was considered to be an expert in the law and by biblical definition was an "expert." He had obviously chosen to overlook the requirement to express love to others who were not identified within his personal, social, or religious context.

How many of us are guilty of expressing love for God only within the circles of those with whom we are personally, socially, and religiously comfortable with, while at the same time overlook ing the needs of others whom the Lord has called us to serve? Our failures to express our love is shown in the magnitude of problems that are manifest throughout the world. It is seen in the faces of the children starving in the Sudan, the displaced in Rwanda, the distraught in Bosnia, the disappointed and distressed in America's urban centers, the hopeless who have been left behind in rural America, and the hapless who work every day, but still cannot get above the poverty line.

The lawyer, uncomfortable with the reflection of himself in the mirror of interpretation and in an attempt to justify himself, asks Jesus, "And who is my neighbor?" Jesus responds by offering the oft quoted parable, which is referred to as the parable of the good Samaritan. The parable presents several classes of people who are expected by their calling, profession, and commitment to be responsive to human needs as an expression of God's love for all humanity. He presents the story of a man going down from Jerusalem to Jericho who fell into the hands of robbers. The route that the man has taken is a common one, known for its danger to the degree that often it is called "The Way of Blood." It is like many of the streets in our communities, subways, and other places where our people travel daily. He had been robbed, stripped of his clothes, beaten, and left for dead. A priest, who probably traveled this road often, saw the man and in spite of his condition, passed on the other side. Jesus points to the indifference and lack of love and compassion shown by this religious man. How could a person who is called to religious ministry show such insensitivity and lack of compassion to another human being?

Haven't we all been guilty at some point in our life of passing a stranger in need because we are afraid of getting involved? But worse than that, some of us are so religious that we cannot even speak to another human being. God has called us to be the priest showing mercy and selflessness in response to other human beings and to human need. This was an opportunity for service that was overlooked by the priest. He probably assumed that he had fulfilled all of his religious requirements to God before leaving the temple. You cannot leave the love of God in the church, you must take it to the streets. He failed miserably in fulfilling his religious requirement to suffering humanity. The love of God transcends the limitations of the places where we worship as evidenced by Jesus' parable of the sheep and goats, when he declares, *"I tell you the truth, whatever you did not do to the least of these, you did not do for me"* (Matthew 25:45). We are continually challenged to share God's love with the hungry, the thirsty, the stranger, the naked, the sick, and the incarcerated.

Secondly, there was a Levite, a brother beloved in the temple, who had fulfilled his responsibility of the preparation of the temple for worship and sacrifice. He was held in high esteem in the temple. However, when he came to the man who had been robbed, mugged, and left for dead, he saw him, but moved to the other side of the road. He couldn't pretend that he did not know that the man needed help: He <u>saw</u> him. Many of us have been guilty of making the separation between our worship and our service.

The Levite was not curious enough to see if he could help the man who had been brutally victimized by the robbers. He did not realize that this was an opportunity that God had presented him to manifest in a real way the piety that he had shown while in the temple? Even if he had not been a Levite, it seems as if there should have been a thread of human compassion that would have forced him to respond to the needs of a dying man. Could it be that he had traveled this road so long and had seen so many others in the same pitiful condition that he had become indifferent to their suffering and pain?

I am amazed at the tolerance and acceptance that are shown by persons who live daily amid the fatalism, brutality, robbing, and murders that have wrecked our communities. Children are dying without having had a chance to live, and often the response of the Church is silence. <u>Where is the love</u> that should be the mark of our Christian responsibility and service? Don't we realize that today it may be someone else's child that is killed, but tomorrow it could be our child? Many teenagers have been to more funerals by the time they are eighteen than most adults who have lived to become senior citizens. There is obviously a crying need to respond to the pain and suffering of those who are the survivors, yet I tend to believe that more often than not, the Christian response is to give lip service rather than tender love to those who have been victimized. Thus, many of the young people who do survive the streets, schools, and playgrounds of our communities have no use for the church, because they do not see our love for one another or for them. They have lost any hope or belief that they will live to become adults and do not believe that the church cares one way or the other. Where is the love?

Recent articles suggest that some of our children have already planned their funerals by the time they enter junior high school. We must love and nurture our youth since they have become the primary victims of the robbers, murderers, muggers, and thieves. The standard of love that Christ gives us in his command, "Love each other as I have loved you," must become the standard for everyone who follows his teachings. Where is the love?

Many young babies get pregnant and have babies in their search for love only to discover that they lack the discipline to raise a child. Young boys, some reared without a father in the home, and others reared with a father, some of whom are abusive, seek love in gangs and pay the ultimate price through either incarceration or death. Where is the positive love that seems so elusive, the tough love that seems so necessary, the Christian love that could make a difference in their lives? Churches who analyze these problems must ask themselves, "Where is the love?"

The third man, a Samaritan traveling the same road, but not a member of the temple because of his race, understood the principle of love. Although he was clearly not to be classified as a brother of the sufferer by virtue of his ethnicity, in a region that discriminated against him did understand what it meant to show compassion for another human being. He, by definition, was hated by the Jews, but never asked the racial or ethnic background of the man who was dying. He saw the same bloody, limp, dying form of a man, wounded and near death, lying by the wayside, that the priest and Levite had seen, but instead of ignoring the man's plight, he was moved to show kindness and love. He stayed with the wounded man, knowing that on this "Way of Blood," his own life could be in peril. He gave his best effort to assist this helpless soul. With unselfish, brotherly love, he tenderly bandaged the man, poured the balm of oil and wine on him, and then made the sacrifice of giving up his own seat on his donkey to carry the man into the city for additional care. He showed even greater love and benevolence the next day when he took out two silver coins to pay the innkeeper saying, "When I return, I will reimburse you for any extra expense you may have." Jesus completed the parable and looked at the lawyer and asked the question, "Which now of these three do you think was a neighbor to the man who fell into the hands of the robbers?" The expert in the law replied, "The one who had mercy upon him."

We as Christians are called upon to do as the Samaritan, showing our love and compassion to those who are in need. Our roles and responsibilities do not end when the benediction has been pronounced at the conclusion of worship. Rather, after worship, our service begins and is expressed through our love, our human sympathy and compassion in response to the commandment of God. The Lord compels us to love all humanity without qualification. Jesus declares in John 15:9: *"As the Father has loved me, so have I loved you. Now remain in my love."* Love has everything to do with the fulfillment of our Christian commitments as a reciprocal response to the love of Christ Jesus. II Corinthians 5:14 says, *"For Christ's love compels us because we are convinced that one died for all and therefore all died."* Since Christ has died for us as the ultimate expression of love, and compels us to remain in His love, we are challenged to demonstrate that love in how we treat other people. We are reminded that our love for Christ is inseparable from our actuating that love through our commitments and response to human need.

The government may not be as compassionate as we desire, in spite of that we are called to remain committed to love one another as the Lord has loved us; politicians may be brutal in their assaults on programs that help the needy; nevertheless, we who are in the body of Christ, whether rich or poor, black or white, Jew or Gentile, must be reminded that God's love has been given for each one of us. It is God's unchangeable love that represents the foundation for unity in a fractured world. Divisiveness, strife, poverty, war, and humanity's crying needs can all be addressed through our love for Christ and for one another.

The apostle Paul raised several relevant questions in Romans

8:35–39: *"Who shall separate us from the love of Christ? Shall trouble or hardship or persecution or famine or nakedness or danger or sword? As it is written, for thy sake we are killed all the day long; we are accounted as sheep for the slaughter."* He answers the questions by declaring, *"Nay, in all these things we are more than conquerors through him that loved us. For I am persuaded, that neither death, nor life, nor angels, nor principalities, nor powers, nor things present, nor things to come, nor height, nor depth nor any other creature, shall be able to separate us from the love of God, which is in Christ Jesus our Lord."*

In order to fulfill our Christian commitment, we must express the power of God's love in all things that we do. *"Keep yourself in God's love as you wait for the mercy of our Lord Jesus Christ to bring you to eternal life"* (Jude 21). Where is the love? Love becomes real when we are following God's commands, honoring our faith commitment to Christ, and fulfilling our service requirements to humanity. This is how we know what love is: *"Jesus Christ laid down His life for us and we ought to lay down our life for others"* (I John 3:16). *"For God so loved the world that he gave His only begotten Son, that whosoever believeth in him should not perish but have everlasting life"* (John 3:16). God's love has lifted us so that we can express our love by lifting others and making plain the perfect nature of God's love to all humanity and bringing life, hope, and meaning to all who join in the joyous hymn that proclaims:

O perfect love all human thought transcending,
Lowly we kneel in prayer before thy throne,
That theirs may be a love that knows no ending,
Whom thou forevermore dost join in one.

O perfect life, be thou their full assurance
Of tender charity and steadfast faith,
Of patient hope and quiet, brave endurance,
With childlike trust that fears no pain nor death.

Grant them the joy which brightens earthly sorrow;
Grant them the peace which calms all earthly strife,
And to life's day the glorious unknown morrow
That dawns upon eternal love and life. Amen.

Where is the love? It is in the maternity wards of hospitals, where volunteers take time to hold little babies who have been born of drug addiction for a few hours each day. It is found in the community, where attempts are made to provide services to the poor and homeless. It is expressed through the hearts and intelligence of those who volunteer to tutor and mentor our youth. It is in evidence at churches where food, clothing, shelter, and other resources are made available to those who are needy. It is shown at the cross where Christ made the ultimate sacrifice of love by dying for all humanity. It is made manifest at the tomb, where the dead are given new life at the appointed time of the resurrection of Jesus Christ. Where is the love? It is in your heart and my heart and the hearts of all who express the love of God to all humanity regardless of race, class, gender, or religious persuasion.

A NEW COMMANDMENT
Jeremiah A. Wright, Jr.

This uplifting Maundy Thursday sermon extols and explains God's commandment for us to love one another. We are informed that love means forgetting, forgiveness, trust, and hard work.

JOHN 13:25–35

I'D LIKE YOU to look along with me as we examine John 13:25–35. Let us read:

"So while reclining next to Jesus, he asked him, 'Lord, who is it?' Jesus answered, 'It is the one to whom I give this piece of bread when I dip it in the dish.' After he received the piece of bread, Satan entered into him. Jesus said to him, 'Do quickly what you are going to do.' Now no one at the table knew why he said this to him. Some thought that because Judas had the common purse, Jesus was telling him to buy what we need for the festival or that he should give something to the poor. So, after receiving the piece of bread, he immediately went out, and there was night. When he had gone out, Jesus said, 'Now the Son of Man has been glorified, and God has been glorified in you dear little children. I am only with you a little longer. You will look for me, as I said to the Jews, so now I say to you, where I am going, you cannot come. I give you a new commandment that you love one another, just as I have loved you. You also should love one another. By this everyone will know that you are my disciples.'"

Tonight, the night on which the Lord was betrayed. Tonight, the night on which after observing the Passover supper, the Lord Jesus then instituted the Lord's supper. Tonight, as Jesus and those whom he loved gathered in a room to enjoy a special moment together, a moment of remembrance, a moment of thanksgiving and a moment of joy—tonight. I wonder if you realize how important tonight is? Each year I have grown more and more appalled as I have watched who came and who did not come to the Maundy Thursday service, the services which mark the beginning of the climax of the Lord's earthly work. There was a minister who shared a ride with me from the airport on Maundy Thursday. I asked him, "Are you going back for service tonight at your church, Doc?" He said, "No, we had service Monday, Tuesday, and Wednesday." I said, "What about tonight?" He responded, "No, we're having them tomorrow, Good Friday."

We use this weekend as a time to go shopping, and partying, and as a time to relax. Some businesses are closed tomorrow. Some schools are closed tomorrow. Our minds are on movies and Marshall Fields' spring sales and Easter bunnies, when our minds need to be on what the Lord did *tonight*. What happened to the Lord tonight? What happened to him early in the morning on Friday, from nine in the morning until three in the afternoon? Tonight is when he said, "This, do in remembrance of me." And tonight is when every Christian church in the country should be packed out with standing room only.

I watched last year as our teenagers, leaving their rehearsal on Maundy Thursday, were going to McDonald's when they should have been heading for the sanctuary to fall on their knees for what the Lord had done for them. I thought about the difference between Jewish teenagers and black Christian teenagers. And then I thought about the difference between the parents of Jewish teenagers and the parents of black Christian teenagers. I can't hold the kids accountable for what the parents haven't taught them. It's not the kid's fault, it's the parent's fault. How many black children in this church know what tonight means? Not many in the community, or in this church, know what happened tonight. I don't mean how many black kids in the *world* know. I mean how many black kids in this congregation know? I heard our choir director ask the choir members almost apologetically on Monday night to please come out and observe the religious holiness of this day. After rehearsing every night last week, working hard for six hours on a musical project on Monday night, they had to be invited to participate with the rest of the congregation on this night, when the fact of the matter is, if it wasn't for this night they wouldn't have anything to sing about those other nights.

I have watched in horror at how lightly we take this night when

this is one of the most important nights on the entire Christian cal-
endar. At least twelve times a year, and for some of us, like the
deacons, three times every first Sunday, thirty-six times a year,
you hear the minister say, "On the night on which he was betrayed, after supper he took bread," and this is the night the minister's talking about — tonight, as Jesus and those he loved gathered
in a room to enjoy a precious moment together; tonight, the same
night he laughed in a relaxed moment and cried in a wrenching
moment; tonight, the same night he experienced betrayal by one
whom he trusted.

Have you ever been betrayed? You ever have somebody you
love betray your trust? Have you ever been hurt deeply by somebody you love? This is the night that Jesus experienced what he
expected. This is the night that Jesus said, "Do what you got to
do," and Judas went and sold him out. This is the night that the
one he loved turned him over to the ones who hated him; the one
he loved smiled at him and kissed him — and it turned out to be a
kiss of death. This is the same night he prayed more passionately
than he had ever prayed. Have you ever prayed so hard that you
started crying while you were praying? Jesus did. Have you ever
prayed so intensely that God had to send an angel to minister to
you in your misery? Jesus did. Have you ever been hurt so bad
that you thought the hurt would never heal? Jesus was — tonight,
the same night he prayed in the Garden and was betrayed in the
Garden. Tonight, as Jesus and those he loved gathered in the
room to enjoy a precious moment together, Jesus gave a new commandment, that I want to examine with you for a few moments if
you will allow me.

A new commandment. Jesus said in so many words, I know
you know the other commandments. I've been watching you for
three years now. I know you know the *Ten Commandments*. I see
how you live and I know what you do. Now I have another commandment. I've got a new commandment — a new commandment
give I unto you.

Tonight, Jesus gave us (me and you) a new commandment
which in many ways took the requirements of discipleship a notch
higher. Look at how God works. You know the Lord just loves the

number three. The combination of three. Theologians say the very
number three is the God number. God in three persons, blessed
trinity. God the father, *one;* God the son, *two;* God the holy ghost,
three. In Genesis 18, when Abraham looked up he saw *three* men
walking up to his tent door; when the history of the patriarchs is
rehearsed; and even when God, God's self, confronts Moses on a
mountain in Midian and the historian says what God says; the
partriarchs were Abraham, Isaac, and Jacob—*three.* The Lord
says, "I am the God of Abraham, Isaac, and Jacob"—*three.* When
Solomon built the temple for the worship of the Lord, he planted
it in a city, Jerusalem, whose walls were like the walls of the New
Jerusalem. They had *three* gates in the east, and *three* gates in the
west, and *three* gates in the north, and *three* gates in the south—
God specializes in the number three.

When God wanted to show King Nebuchadnezzar that the father was more powerful than the fire, he chose Shadrach, Me-
shach, and Abednego. He not only demonstrated that, but he also
showed him how prayer was more powerful than politics. When
Jonah tried to get away from God, God took him on a detour in
the belly of a whale for *three* days. When the seraphim sang out in
Isaiah 6, what did they say? HOLY (one), HOLY (two), HOLY
(three) IS THE LORD, GOD OF HOSTS. Heaven and earth
are full of thy glory. God specializes in this number three!

When God wanted to demonstrate God's power over impossible gynecological conditions, He chose Sarah, past menopause,
and he put a baby in her womb. (That's One!) He chose Eliza-
beth, also past menopause, and He put a baby in her womb. (That's
Two!) Then, He chose Mary, a virgin, and put the Son of God in
her womb. (That's Three!) Theology overruled gynecology.

When the Magi came to worship him, when he was born King
of the Jews, they brought gold (that's one), frankincense (that's
two), and myrrh, *three* gifts for the Light of the World. When
Jesus chose an inner circle, brothers who would pray privately
with him, brothers who would approach the presence of God with
him and brothers who would stay with him, and stand with him
through thick and thin, who did he choose? Peter, James, and
John—THREE. When it came to those whom he loved, dearly,

folk in whose home he could rest his head, folk at whose table he could eat his fill, folk with whose hearts he could share his dreams, who did he choose? Mary, Martha, and Lazarus—THREE.

When he wanted to demonstrate his power over death, he raised a Jairus' daughter in Capernaum (that's one), he raised the widow's son in Nain (that's two); and then he brought back Lazarus from a four-day grave in Bethany. That was three. When they put him on a cross to crucify him for crimes that you and I committed, the sun in the sky looked down on the son in Calvary and refused to shine from twelve until three—THREE HOURS.

When he went in the grave, he stayed there on Friday—one. He stayed there on Saturday—two. But my Bible tells me that early on the *third* day, with all power in his hand, he got up to give us the victory! God specializes in three.

And when it came to commandments, what did Jesus already say? The greatest commandment is that thou shalt love the Lord thy God with all thy heart, with all thy soul, with all thy mind, with all thy strength—that's one. That's the greatest command-ment. He said the second is, "Thou shalt love thy neighbor as thyself"—that's two. But then when it came to the new command-ment which would be number three, God pulled out all the stops. He makes this the requirement for being a disciple. "By this every-one shall know that you are my disciples." Love God. That's one. Love thy neighbor as you love yourself. That's two. Then, love one another. A new commandment give I unto you—Love one another as I have loved you.

Notice also, if you will, that love is not an option. Turn to your neighbor and say, "Love is not an option." Turn back and tell them, "It's a requirement." He makes the requirements even harder. Notice how all three of the commandments have loving in them. Not hate. Not vengeance. Not payback. But Love.

Love is not something you *can* do or can*not* do depending on how you're feeling. Love is not an elective that you can take or skip depending on how full your plate is or how crowded your schedule is or how much else you got to do or what you think is important. Love is not a take-it-or-leave-it kind of possibility. Love is not one choice among many in a multiple-choice game. Love is the only choice you've got if you're going to be one of the disciples. Love is the only game in God's town. *Love* the Lord your God with all your heart, mind, and strength; *Love* your neighbor as you love yourself; and *Love* one another. Not an abstract neighbor somewhere, but a concrete person—a disciple—someone working with you and walking with you. Not a nebulous anybody, but an up-close somebody. We're talking about the one you sit beside in church—and can't stand. You go all out of your way to keep from speaking to them. Love that one. The one you lay beside at night who gets on your last nerve. That's the one. Love that one! Love one another as I have loved you. This is the new commandment, and this is the one to me that is the most difficult commandment of all.

You see "love," especially love like the Lord's love for us, means forgiving. It is a constant theme in the Lord's teaching, something that most of us have a terrible time doing. "We don't get mad, we get even." That's what we say. That's what we do. Payback is a boogerbear. But what does the Lord say? "Don't get even, get over it." Forgive.

I was talking to a brother this week, a beautiful brother, a strong brother, an African-American warrior brother. And this brother told me that he had been mad at me for two and a half years. Something I said he misunderstood, two and a half years ago. We hold on to stuff and hold on to it and hold on to it and all it does is eat us up. The other person has gone on with their lives, forgotten all about it, and we are still stuck right there. I didn't have the slightest clue, first of all, that I had upset the brother until he brought it to my attention this week. Second of all, it reminded me of something I thought he and his wife had settled a long time ago. But then most of all, I couldn't even remember for the life of me what in the world he was talking about. I had forgotten about it and moved on and he was still right there, stuck in that same spot for two and a half years. He was still mad thirty months later!

Love means forgiving, and forgiving is not something we do too easily. How many times have you heard people say, "Reverend, I might be able to forgive, but I sure as hell ain't gonna forget." I've got a hot flash for you—FORGIVING *IS* FORGETTING!

Those of you who have your Bible, turn right quick to Jeremiah 31:34 and hear what God has to say. Don't believe what Jeremiah Wright has to say, listen to God. It says, "I will forgive their iniquity and I will remember their sin no more." Repeat God's word after me: "I will forgive their iniquity and I will remember their sin no more." Repeat God's word after me: "I will forgive their iniquity and I will remember their sin no more."

LOVE MEANS FORGIVING AND FORGETTING. I have shared with our congregation the story of a woman who told her pastor that God talked directly to her in a clear voice every now and then and she kept on worrying her pastor, "Reverend, God came into my bedroom last night and he talked to me again. He told me exactly what was going to happen today, what you were going to preach, and what the choir was going to sing." And her pastor thought that she wasn't playing with a full deck. (You do know that we get all kinds at the church house. Almost every Sunday night, at the six o'clock service there is a brother here waiting to see me to talk about absolutely nothing, pure "D" insanity. Every week he plays crazy to ask me for money. We get all kinds at the church house. One brother comes in on crutches every week trying to get a free feel. Some want free wheels, some want free meals, some want free feels.) Her pastor thought that she was a few slices short of a full loaf. So, he would just put up with her and say something polite to her and go to his office, as nice as he could, each week, till she said the Lord had spoken to her, and told her something about him. And he said, "I don't think so; God doesn't operate like that."

"Oh yes, he did."

"I don't think so."

"Oh yes, he did."

"I don't think so."

"Oh yes, he did."

Then Reverend said, "Tell you what, if God told you something about me, the next time the Lord comes into your room, you ask Him, what sin did I commit on New Year's Eve of 1993?" She said "Okay, fine." The next Sunday, she was right there. She said, "Reverend, I asked him and he told me." And Reverend was taken by surprise. She caught him off guard and just in case she really did talk to God and God really did talk back to her, he didn't want her to blurt it out right there in the doorway, with all the people in line standing there. So he said, "Well, heh, heh, heh." (That's one of those don't-be-tickled laughs.) "Go to my office and wait for me. I'll be there in a few moments."

He finished shaking hands at the door, but every time he said, "God bless you" to a member, he kept asking himself, "I wonder if God really told her. I wonder who she talked to to find out. She couldn't. How does she know? How *much* does she know?" When the last member left, he walked to his office in terror. What was going to happen if this woman really knew?

He got there and he asked her, "You talked to God? God came in your bedroom? What did you ask God?" "Exactly what you told me to ask him." "And what was that?"—hoping she got it mixed up, that he was going to fix this thing and get out of it good. She said, "I asked him what sin you committed on New Year's Eve of 1993."

"And God answered you?"

"UH-HUH."

"What did God say?" he asked.

She broke into a wide grin and said, "God said I can't remember."

"I will forgive their iniquity and I will remember their sin no more!!!" Love means forgiving and forgetting! Love means letting go of it! And forgetting it! The only way you can get *over* it is to let *go* of it. Just this week, folk got mad, uptight, upset, jaws locked, bona fide 'tudes over the CD that the choir cut. Who said what? Who did what? Who got to come in early? Who didn't? Who she think she is? Jesus said forgive, people make mistakes. Everybody makes mistakes. I make mistakes, and guess what? Even YOU make mistakes! But we come from a culture that says, "If they make mistakes, get 'em." Jesus says, however, "Forgive them." Love means forgiving, and that ain't easy.

Jesus takes the requirement for kingdom residence up a notch. Love means forgiving and then love means trusting. For many of us that ain't easy either. Jesus said love one another. And that not only means forgive one another, but also trust one another. Let me tell you something about this trusting business. When you've been burnt one time, it's hard to trust. When you've been burnt two times, it's well nigh into impossible for some of us to trust. Come on and say Amen if you know what I'm talking about. But, then when it is more than two times that somebody has betrayed your trust, it's three strikes and you're out. It's all over. Forget it. Throw it out of your mind. That is how we operate, but guess what? That is not how God operates. The Lord just keeps on giving us chance after chance after chance. Aren't you glad about it? If it hadn't been for God giving you another chance, you would not be here tonight. If it hadn't been for the Lord trusting you when you said, "God, I'm sorry, give me just one more chance. Try me one more time," we'd all have flunked out by now. But he trusts us even when our track record is poor.

I have a psychologist friend who is a Christian psychologist. He was telling me how he shocked this couple who was working with him in therapy. One of the mates felt, "You have blown it and you've got to earn my trust if you ever want me to trust you again." And the other mate felt, "I really have blown it. I'm on probation and now I've got to prove my worthiness to be trusted because I know my mate ain't going to trust until I show him something." And the psychologist said, "No, you are both wrong. You don't have to earn trust and you don't have to prove yourself." To trust someone is a decision you make based on no proof, no guarantee, no safeguards, no earning of it. It's like grace. You decide to freely give it. That's how the Lord gave his trust to us. A new commandment, give I unto you that you love one another as I have loved you. Forgive one another as I have forgiven you. Trust one another as I have trusted you. While we were yet sinners—we hadn't done a thing to earn anything—while we were yet sinners, Christ died for us. It's a decision he made. He decided to die just to save me. Love means forgiving and love means to trust and both of those add up to the third thing, which is this: Love means hard work.

Now some of you used to hear that sung in doo-wops and didn't know what you were listening to. In fact some of you used to sing along with it. You all remember Junior Walker and the All-Stars. When he found out it was hard work, he used to say, "Love, who needs it? Just to live a life free and easy." Don't look at me like I'm crazy. You all know that song. "Love, who needs it? Just to live a life free and easy. Put the toothbrush in my hand. And let me be a travelin' man."

See, he wants to keep movin' because he knows if he stays there he's gonna have to do some hard work. Who needs hard work? He doesn't want that. Love means HARD WORK. That's why it's a mandate. A new order. A new commandment. I'm not giving you any choice in this matter. This is hard work. Love means, "This is not necessarily something that I *want* to do. This is something that I've *got* to do." Love is an act of the will. That is why when I marry couples, you never hear them say "I do." I don't ask them anything about "do." I say *will* you and if so say "I will," because it is an act of the will.

And don't get confused—it ain't about feelings. It isn't about warm fuzzies all the time either. Love means even when I *don't* feel—especially when I don't feel like it. Even when she gets on my last nerve, and I get on hers. Even when you don't feel like it. Jesus this night didn't feel like going to the cross. Jesus this night didn't feel like going through the crucifixion. Jesus just knew God could come up with some other plan. "Father," he prayed, "if it's possible take this cup away from me." I don't feel like *this*. Matthew said he prayed that prayer *three* times—(there's that number three again). Jesus this night didn't feel like going through what he had to go through in order to bring us through. But love is not a matter of how you feel.

Even though he didn't feel like it, Jesus went to Calvary to save a wretch like you and me—now that's love. Love one another as I have loved you. Love even when you don't feel like it. "They hung him high, they stretched him wide." Love even when it doesn't feel good to you. "They hung him high, they stretched him wide, he hung his head, for me he died." That's what love is! You want to know what love is? Love one another as I have loved you! Forgive them, father, for they know not what they do! Love means trust and occupy until I come! Peter, feed my sheep. Upon this rock, I build my church; I leave with them my peace. Love means hard work, and with pain shooting through every cell of his body,

He hung there, deserted by all but a few;

He hung there, lied on by those he loved;

He hung there, denied by the one he trusted;

He hung there while they teased him;

He hung there while they made fun of him;

He hung there until the veil of the temple tore itself in two;

He hung there until the sun went out;

He hung there until the moon dripped away in blood;

He hung there until the dead in Jerusalem got up and walked;

He hung there until justice was satisfied;

He hung there until all the accounts were settled;

He hung there until salvation was established and redemption was secure;

He hung there until heaven couldn't take it any longer. That's love. For us he died. Now that's love.

But that's not the end of the story. On the third day, he rose again. That's love. That's love. That's love.

LIBERATING LOVE: PASS IT ON
Toinette M. Eugene

*Using Dr. Martin Luther King, Jr., and the prophet Elijah
as catalyst, this sermon advises us that we are recipients of
God's greatest gift and that we are to treasure it, exalt it,
and share it for the betterment of all people and the creation
of Dr. King's beloved community.*

II KINGS 2:4–15

A Double Portion

Elisha had been the protégé of Elijah. He was familiar with and impressed by what Elijah had done. Elijah had faced the awesome power of King Ahab and had dared to pronounce, in the presence of the royal court, the wickedness of the monarch. For Ahab had exercised the regal power of eminent domain and had confiscated the vineyard of a poor peasant. Elijah brought God's judgment into the royal court. In the presence of false prophets Elijah called upon his God for a sign of favor and vocation. And God set wet wood on fire.

Elijah was indeed a chosen one. But there was also the occasion when Elijah's enemies sought his life, and Elijah, giving in to despair, sat down and wept under the juniper tree. Yet, God cured Elijah's blues. God refreshed and revitalized the prophet, giving him renewed vigor and commitment. Surely, in their many days together these and other testimonies were shared with Elisha. But the time came when God called Elijah home from the battlefield.

Looking down upon the prophet whose days had been spent in the pursuit of justice and righteousness, God's voice rolled down the streets of Glory. Forth came a chariot of fire with flaming steeds, which had waited since creation for this moment. I can almost hear God saying, "I want you to go down to Jericho. I'm calling Elijah home. He's held fast to the gospel plow; now I'm calling him home. He's fought the good fight on the mountain and in the valley; now I'm calling him home. He has run the race, finished the course, and now it's time for him to receive his crown.

I'm calling him home. He'll meet you at the Jordan River. Go and bring my servant home."

But before Elijah left for Glory, he turned to his friend Elisha and said, "Ask what I shall do for you before I am taken from you." What can I do for you before I go? Out of all of the things for which Elisha could have asked, he chose this: "Let me inherit a double portion of your spirit." Whatever it was that put the truth on your tongue and righteousness in your heart, give me a double portion. Whatever it was that made justice your defense and love your way, give me a double portion of it. Elisha asked for a double portion, not because Elisha wanted to be twice as famous as Elijah, but because evil stalked the earth and plagued the human heart day and night.

Some of us may be familiar with the sermon that Martin Luther King, Jr., preached on the eve of his assassination. With the fire of divine inspiration in his eyes he said, "There are difficult days ahead . . . [but] I'm not worried about anything. I'm not fearing anyone. Mine eyes have seen the glory of the coming of the Lord. . . . I have been to the mountaintop, and I have looked over into the Promised Land." If there is one thing that we need today it is a double portion of Dr. King's spirit. Whatever it was that made him call the demons of racism, militarism, and oppression by name, we need a double portion. Whatever it was that made him stand up against fire hoses, billy clubs, physical and verbal abuse for righteousness' sake, we need a double portion. A double portion, not because we want twice the notoriety of Martin Luther King, but because he has told us that there are difficult days ahead.

I suppose if Dr. King were here today he would respond to us in the way that Elijah responded to the request of Elisha: "You have asked me a hard thing," or "Do you know what that means? For along with the double portion comes more than your share of trouble. Are you ready to be rejected for no other cause than that your skin is black? Are you ready to be persecuted for no other cause than that you cry out for justice in behalf of the downtrodden? Are you prepared to go to battle against the forces of war with nothing but the weapons of peace? You are asking a hard thing." If we want a double portion of Dr. King's spirit today, we must be ready to accept all of its implications. The light of truth will not shine brightly until we name it. The power of justice will not cleanse us until we live it. The joy of righteousness will not be ours until we believe it.

Spiritual Insight

Elisha asked for a double portion of Elijah's spirit, but it was not completely within Elijah's power to grant the request. The spirit that Elijah had did not alter his physical makeup. It did not change the tonal quality of his voice. In fact, there was nothing about the prophetic spirit that was obvious to the casual observer. The only test that would answer Elisha's question was the possession of a spiritual insight. Elijah told him, "You have asked a hard thing, yet if you see me as I am being taken from you, it shall be so for you; but if you do not see me, it shall not be so."

Elisha may have already had his double portion, but in order to be sure, he had to see with the eyes of faith. We—you and I today—may already have our double portion, but to be certain we have to see with the eyes of faith. We have to be able to see in Afro-Americans the heritage of a noble African culture. But in order to see that we have to look with what the old folks call the spiritual eye.

For in the economic eye, Afro-Americans are simply surplus labor. In the political eye, Afro-Americans are simply surplus votes. In the social eye, Afro-Americans are merely a burden on society, but in the spiritual eye . . . in the spiritual eye these are they who have come up out of the great tribulation. In the spiritual eye, these are they who have formed mighty civilizations. In the spiritual eye, these are they upon whose blood this land is built. In the spiritual eye, these are they who are denied equal opportunity and the pursuit of happiness. In the spiritual eye, these are they who are destined for a place in God's house. We have to see with the spiritual eye.

We have to look behind the gleaming facade of corporate

America and see persons consumed by their own greed. We have to see with the spiritual eye. We have to look beneath the manicured surface of American society and see people numbed by rampant apathy. We have to look beyond the attractive frontier of American military conquest and see a world in danger of nuclear annihilation. We need the spiritual eye! The spirit of prophecy is ineffective without the insight of faith. We cannot just cry out for justice but we need to have seen it from afar. We cannot just demand the righteousness but we must believe it. We cannot just pray for peace but we must be able to see the things that make peace possible.

In a speech that Martin Luther King delivered at the Riverside Church, he said, "A nation that continues year after year to spend more money on military defense than on programs of social uplift is approaching spiritual death. . . . Somehow this madness must cease." King saw with the spiritual eye the malaise of our country. If we want to redeem it, we need the spirit of prophecy and the eyes of faith.

Pass It On

Elisha was granted his wish. He received a double portion of the spirit of Elijah. The spirit of prophecy rested on him. And he was also endowed with spiritual insight with the eyes of faith. As the chariot of fire swung low he saw Elijah being taken up to heaven. He saw for himself the whirlwind that carried God's servant to his final and eternal reward. Elisha had the gift of prophecy and the eyes of faith, but the question still remained: Would he be able to pass it on? Would he be able to do for Israel what Elijah had done for him? Would he be able to pass on to the people the hope that had sustained Elijah?

Israel was the heir of a glorious history. Abraham had been summoned to be the founder of a great nation. Isaac prospered under God's favor. Jacob was blessed even when he did not deserve it. Joseph, sold by his brothers into Egyptian slavery, became respected among the pharaohs. And when God delivered

Israelites from bondage in Egypt they took the bones of Joseph with them. In Israel's past lay her heritage and her hope. But something had happened to Israel. They forgot God's promise. They neglected God's command. They were unable to pass on to succeeding generations the liberating love that inspired their ancestors.

If there is one thing that has plagued black people, as well as many other religiously oriented people in America, it is the inability to consistently pass on our history. An inability to leave for future generations a heritage of hope and a legacy of love. It is a history held together by the demand for justice and a thirst after righteousness. In the lives and accomplishments of Nat Turner, Harriet Tubman, Richard Allen, Jarena Lee, Sojourner Truth, Augustus Tolton, Malcolm X, and all of the others, we can see the results of a prophetic call. The tragedy is that we have shown a disdain for our noble history and have failed to pass it on! The redemption of our race and our nation may rest on our ability to give to our children what we have received.

The Afro-American writer Toni Morrison in her novel *Song of Solomon* tells the story of an ex-slave whose farm embodies his heritage. The farm says, "Stop picking around the edges of the world. Take advantage, and if you can't take advantage, take disadvantage. . . . Grab this land! Take it, hold it, my brothers, make it, my sisters; shake it, squeeze it, turn it, twist it, beat it, kick it, kiss it, whip it, stomp it, dig it, plow it, seed it, reap it, rent it, buy it, sell it, own it, build it, multiply it, and pass it on—can you hear me? Pass it on!"

Elijah did not leave Elisha empty-handed, wondering whether or not he would be able to pass on to others the prophetic inheritance. No! As Elijah was being taken up, he looked over his shoulder and flung his mantle down toward Elisha. The mantle was a symbol of the prophetic vocation. It had no power in and of itself, but it served as a reminder of the God who protected him in danger, fed him when he was hungry, gave him drink when he was thirsty.

Martin Luther King, Jr., as he was being taken up to glory, in the midst of his eschatological joy, seeing our trepidation and fear, looked over his shoulder and flung down his mantle. He gave us his dream. A dream of justice and equality. The dream has no power in and of itself, but it is a reminder of the God who made a way out of no way, the God who has delivered us from bondage, the God who has opened doors that no one can close. No! Martin Luther King has not left us empty-handed but has given us something to hold on to. He has passed on to us his dream.

Conclusion

Elisha was left standing on the bank of the Jordan. He had in his hand Elijah's mantle. It was the same mantle with which Elijah had parted the waters. A mantle that was itself a reminder of the rod with which Moses had parted the Red Sea. But all of that was past and Elisha now faced the uncertain future. And the question that must have haunted his mind is, "Can we do it again? Can I part the water with Elijah's mantle?" As we face our uncertain future we may also be wondering whether or not we can weather the winter of persecution. Can we once again articulate a vision of the beloved community?

Elisha discovered that with the mantle of Elijah he could strike the waters of the Jordan and part them. With Dr. King's dream we can continue to work effectively for his beloved community, "where all God's children, black and white, Jews and Gentiles, Protestant and Catholic, will be able to join hands and sing the spiritual of old, 'Free at last! Free at last! Thank God almighty, we are free at last.' " We can part the Red Seas of the world again, we can defeat the pharaohs of this world again, we can dream again, because the power behind Elijah's mantle and dream has become flesh and dwelt among us.

Because the Child of God has taken the form of a slave, because Jesus came into the world of a lowly birth, because he ate with sinners and reprobates, we can dream. Because he befriended the outcasts, championed the cause of the downtrodden, proclaimed the release of the captives, because he has set at liberty those who are oppressed, we are able to act boldly as he did. Because Jesus died the death of a criminal, and assumed the keys of the kingdom, we are set free from sin and called to be disciples. Because Jesus Christ lived, died, and yet lives for us, we can take up Elijah's mantle, and we can live out the courageous spirit of liberation that makes this dream a reality of peace and mercy and justice for our world. We have received God's most precious gift. Liberating Love. Pick it up, take it up, hold it high, and pass it on!

HOW MUCH
DO YOU LOVE JESUS?
Reginald T. Jackson

*Through this provocative message, we are asked to consider
whether we love Jesus more than we love our societal status
and our worldly possessions; equally as important, we are
told to ask ourselves if we love Jesus, as He loved us, greatly
enough to serve God.*

JOHN 21:15

ONE DAY JESUS was passing by the Sea of Galilee and saw two brothers fishing, Peter and his brother Andrew. Jesus said unto them, "Follow me and I will make you fishers of men." They dropped their nets, left their boots, and followed Him. Jesus went on to call others to be apostles, declaring He would make them fishers of man. Over the next three years, these twelve men were to accompany Him as He went about His ministry. They would be closer to Him than anybody. They would be by His side as He performed miracles and taught the masses. Over the three years a bond of love and brotherhood was established between them.

At the end of the three years, when Jesus was crucified out on Calvary, these same apostles were broken and shattered. Their friend, their mentor, their brother and master was dead. How devastated they must have been not only because He died, but also by how He died.

But if they were devastated and shattered over His death, how happy and ecstatic they must have been over His resurrection. Jesus, who had died out on Calvary's hill on Friday, was now alive. They saw Him. Several times they saw Him and talked to Him; on the Emmaus Road, in the Upper Room when Thomas wasn't there and again when Thomas was there. They saw the print of the nails in His hand, and beheld the wound in His side. This was Jesus who died, but rose again. He kept His word. The world couldn't beat Him, death couldn't hold Him, and the grave couldn't keep Him.

One would think that after seeing the risen Christ the apostles would be filled with zeal and passion and set on fire to go out and witness and serve Him; that they would become possessed to go out and win the world for Him. That's what one would think. But instead look at what they did.

In this morning's text, Simon Peter, the spokesman and self-appointed leader of the group, said unto them, "Brothers, I am going fishing." And the other apostles chimed in and said, "We will go fishing also." They went out and got in the ship and went fishing. Notice, if you will, what they did. Three years earlier Jesus had called them from fishing for fish and said unto them, "Follow me and I will make you fishers of men." But now, here they are after His resurrection, going back to their fishing nets, going back to their boats, going back to fishing for fish. Going back to the very thing he had called them from. And they fished all night but they caught nothing, not one fish. And in the morning, Jesus stood on the shore but the apostles didn't know who it was. He said unto them, "Children, have you any meat?" And they answered, "No." And He said to them, "Cast your net on the right side of the ship." And when they did they caught so many fish that their nets were unable to hold them. And the apostle John said to Peter, "It is the Lord." And Peter put on his coat and swam to shore to meet the Lord.

They fixed dinner and Jesus sat down to eat with them. And while they were eating, relaxed and laid back, Jesus asked Peter a most sensitive and penetrating question. "Simon, son of Jonas, lovest thou me more than these?" And Peter responded, "Yes, Lord, you know that I love you." Jesus said unto Him, "Feed my sheep. Simon, son of Jonas, lovest thou me more than these?"

In other words, Peter, how much do you love me? Do you love me more than these? What these? More than the fish of the sea over which you make your living? More than these? More than your nets, more than your bait and tackle, more than your fishing boats? Do you love me more than you love these?

And Peter responded, "Yes, Lord, you know I love you." But that wasn't the first question. The initial question was do you love me more than these. Your lips say yes but your actions say no. For I called you to be fishers of men, but you are out fishing for fish.

How much do you love me? That's what Jesus asks you and me this morning. Not only "Do you love me?" but "How much do you love me?" In your love, where do I rank? Do you love me more than these? These. Those "these" keep messing us up. It's those these that keep coming between us and Jesus. How much do you love me compared with these? And we might ask what "these." We might ask, but we know what the "these" are. Come on, think about it. Do you love him more than things? More than your house, more than your car, more than your jewelry? Do you love me more than your five-figure income and the things that money can buy?

How much do you love me? More than the world and its status and recognition; more than the applause of men and earthly fame; more than your job, more than your friends, more than these? How much do you love me? You testify that I'm your Lord, you sing that I'm all the world to you, you preach that I'm your all, and you say that you are about building my kingdom. But look at you. Your first priority is your own security. What you're building is your own kingdom. You have gone back to what I called you from. You have gone back to being of the world. You are busy looking out for you. But didn't I say, "Seek ye first the kingdom of God and His righteousness and all these other things shall be added unto you?"

How much do we love Jesus? "Lovest thou me more than these?" That's the question. That's the critical point. How well I preach, how well you sing, how well you usher, how well you do whatever you do doesn't matter. What matters is how much do we love Jesus. We talk, we give lip service, we come to church, we shout, we serve on some board or some organization, we are active in the church, we are good members, but how much do we love Jesus? Do we love Him enough to trust Him, do we love Him enough to believe His word, do we love Him enough to tithe, to give our best and do our best for Him? How much do we love Jesus?

Most of us here this morning would declare that we love Jesus more than we do anything. And like Peter, we got offended because somebody asked us. Well, this morning, as an ambassador for Christ I'm asking, how much do we love Jesus?

First, do we love Jesus enough to make Him first in our life? In

other words, do we love Him more than anything? Yes, anything.
To put it another way, more than everything.

Is He our Lord? Lord means number one. Lovest thou me more
than anything. Family, friends, career, job salary, stocks and
bonds. More than welfare, handmade suits, status, position, drugs,
pleasure. Anything, everything, all things, big things, little things,
expensive things, priceless things, these things. Do we love Him
more than anything? Or is there something standing between us
and Him? I love Him more than anything "except." That's not
everything, that's not first. How much do you love Jesus? Do we
love Him enough to be able to stand before God and declare,
"Nothing between my soul and the savior, none of this world's
delusive dream, I have renounced all sinful pleasure, Jesus is
mine, there is nothing between. Nothing between: like worldly
pleasure, habits of life, though harmless they seem, must not my
heart from Him ever sever; He is my all, my Lord, the head of my
life, first, there is nothing between." Do we love Him enough to
make Jesus first in our life?

Second, do we love Jesus enough to serve Him? Not praise
Him, not worship Him, but serve Him. We don't have a problem
praising Him, our problem is serving Him. But if we praise Him
but don't serve Him, we're hypocrites. It's not enough just to
praise Jesus but if we love Him, why not serve Him? A lot of our
praise is lip service. Hot air—all talk, but no action. Jesus wants
us to do with our hands what our hearts find to do. After the benediction, after we get through praising Him, when we get through
telling Him how much we love Him, let us show how much we
love Him by serving Him—in the community, in our schools, in
the courthouses, in our government. In food lines, volunteering at
hospitals. Not with our lips stuck out, not complaining, not grudg-
ingly, not for recognition. But the Word says, "Serve the Lord
with gladness." Do we love Jesus enough to sacrifice some time
and energy serving Him or will we just honor Him with our lips?
How much do we love Jesus? Do we love Him enough to serve
Him?

But finally, maybe I've been asking the wrong questions.
Maybe I need to ask the other question that Jesus asked Peter.

Not how much do we love Jesus but whether we love Jesus at all. Too often we presume that everybody in church loves Jesus. But that's a false presumption. Some don't love Jesus at all. Love the church, but don't love Jesus. Love to have a good time in church, love to sing and show how we can sing, but don't love Jesus. Love to use the church to get some stature and recognition and have a little authority, but don't love Jesus. You know, after all, you can tell when somebody loves you. They don't just tell you, they show you. There's some passion, there's some fire, there's some chemistry, there's some joy. When you love somebody you can't get enough of them.

Jesus didn't just tell us He loved us. He showed us that He loved us. In fact, He showed us how much He loved us. One Friday out on Calvary, He stretched out his arms and He died. Because He loved us, He died. He loved us. He loved us. Every time we see a cross it's a reminder of how much Jesus loved us. There's no doubt about how much He loved us. But the question is, do we love Him? Is there any passion between us and Jesus? Is there any fire, any joy, any chemistry? Can we get enough of Him or do we want more of Him? I hear Him asking, "Do you love me?" And after all, this is a personal question every man must answer for himself. But I tell you whether we answer or not, Jesus knows. Listen to Peter's answer. Lord, you know all things. You know that I love you.

And I'm so glad that Jesus knows that I love Him.

My Jesus, I love thee. I know thou art mine, for thee all the pleasures of sin I resign. My gracious redeemer, my master art thou, if ever I loved thee, my Jesus 'tis now.

TRUE LOVE
Felicia Yvonne Thomas

*How does one recognize true love? In a searching analysis of
II Corinthians, this sermon challenges us to assess the
quality of love in our homes, our personal relationships, our
churches, and our society.*

II CORINTHIANS 11:7–12

L ET THE PEOPLE of God say, "Praise the Lord."

The Lord is good. I'm particularly glad to be here this evening because today I was on the highways, and in the skies in all of that rain. In a teeny-weeny propeller plane. But the Lord is able. And here we stand this evening honoring the God of our Lord and Savior, Jesus Christ.

Won't you pray with me?

We need to hear from you, Lord. We need a word from you. Speak Lord, your servants are listening. Give us ears to hear what your spirit is saying to the church. And now let the words of my mouth, and the collective meditation of our hearts, be acceptable in your sight, O Lord, our rock, and our redeemer. Amen.

It's a privilege to share some thoughts related to the theme: "Growing Together in Christ By Love." For truly, love is the key. In fact, we've been having preaching and praying about love at my church all year long. I'm a new pastor there, in Princeton, at an old church. We just celebrated one hundred and ten years last year and this year the spirit of the Lord spoke to me and said we needed more love. You know, some congregations need more faith. Some need more courage. Some need more patience. I don't mean to imply that in Princeton we don't need those things, but we certainly need more love. Burt Bacharach and Hal David were right when they wrote it, and Dionne Warwick made it plain when she sang it: "What the world needs now is love, sweet love." So, it seems to me that before we can possibly hope or attempt to grow together in love, we need to know what love is. So, this evening, I want to talk about true love. True love.

I want to share with you from the New Testament, the New International Version, from the epistle of Paul, the second epistle to the Corinthian church, chapter 11, verses 7 through 12.

Was it a sin for me to lower myself in order to elevate you by preaching the Gospel of God to you free of charge? I robbed other churches by receiving support from them so as to serve you. And when I was with you and needed something, I was not a burden to anyone. For the brothers who came from Macedonia supplied what I needed. I've kept myself from being a burden to you in any way, and will continue to do so. As surely as the truth of Christ is in me, nobody will stop this boasting of mine in the regions of Achaia. Why? Because I do not love you? God knows I do. And I will keep on doing what I'm doing in order to cut the ground from under those who want an opportunity to be considered equal with us in the things they boast about.

Let's consider for a few moments what Paul has to say about this subject, true love. But in order to understand Paul, we need to shift our attention away from twentieth century Connecticut, and move to first century Corinth in Greece. That's a big switch. It forces us to mentally move some distances. And you all forgive me my liberal education, but I must say this: We, black Baptists, come so close to what Dr. Gardner C. Taylor called biblidolatry. We want to act as though God opened up his mouth and out came the King James Version. But to understand scripture, we must recognize that there is a gulf between us and the words recorded in the book. There is the gulf of geography—because Greece is nothing like Connecticut. There is the space of time and history—because things are different now from how they were in the first century, when the apostle Paul and other apostles, who remained following Jesus' ascension, were trying to found fledgling churches. And then, there is the space of culture—a whole worldview that is so different from ours. We're talking about a time before gravity was discovered; a time before people knew that the earth was round and that the planets revolved around the sun, and not the other way around. So we've got to come a long way to try to approach the scriptures. But you know what? Praise be to God—the more things change, the more they stay the same.

Paul had a love thing going on with the Corinthian church, although the relationship between them was often strained. He did not always like them, but he loved them. And the Corinthians, like some of us today, were their own worst enemies. They were constantly in danger of being led astray by insincere teachers and false doctrine. Their sophistication, wisdom, and worldliness were not always assets. The Corinthian church thought they had it going on, situated as it was right in the heart of the Greco-Roman empire. Corinth was a kind of hub the way that Atlanta is for Delta, and Detroit is for Northwest, and Pittsburgh is for USAir—it was a harbor, it was a crossroads where people converged from all over the empire. If you wanted to go anywhere, chances were you had to go through Corinth. And so, the people there thought that they were sophisticated. They thought that they knew everything and knew everybody. They prided themselves on wisdom. But sometimes, they refused to see the truth because it was just too plain to believe. They did not always trust that "God so loved the world that he gave his only begotten Son; that whosoever believeth in him should not perish, but have everlasting life." No, that was too simple for the Corinthians. They were always looking for something more complicated. They were always looking for something deeper. They were the kind of people who would miss the forest for the trees.

Second Corinthians is a fascinating study in church history and human behavior, because throughout that book, Paul is asserting his own authority. Paul had written to the Corinthians on at least one other occasion. And in closing the book of first Corinthians, Paul had laid out his plans to visit the Corinthian church on his way to Macedonia. As a matter of fact, he was even thinking that he might visit on his way to Macedonia, and then stop back through there when he left Macedonia. But the spirit of the Lord spoke to Paul and told Paul not to do that; so he didn't go.

We see the false apostles getting a hold of this and planting in the church that Paul was wishy-washy; that Paul could not be counted on; that Paul was not true to his word; that Paul did not care for them. You could hear them say, "You all know that Paul. He says one thing, but when push comes to shove, where is he?" Sounds like us. So in this eleventh chapter of second Corinthians, Paul continues his attack on the apostles in the Corinthians' midst. These persons had been maligning Paul's character, questioning his integrity, twisting his teaching, and undermining his authority. Paul had been trying to deal with this situation on the up and up. But the last straw is when these so-called apostles suggest that Paul's teaching is worthless because he is not charging for his services. You know the old saying: "You get what you pay for." When he got on the telephone with them, Paul did not say, "Well, my honorarium is twenty-five hundred dollars. And I got to have a first-class ticket and a limo." The false apostles twisted this around to mean, "What Paul is teaching is worthless—'cause it's free, and everybody knows that nothing for nothing is nothing."

Meanwhile—in the meantime and between time—these so-called self-appointed apostles were pimping and abusing the church for their own gain. And you know, we need to carefully scrutinize folks who would appoint themselves to positions of prominence. I'm not saying that everybody who volunteers and promotes themselves is wrong, but we need to be careful running behind folks who claim, "I got it! I got it! And for twenty-five dollars, you can get it."

Paul's response to the charges that are leveled at him are two-fold. First of all, he speaks the truth in love, even when it's not the nice or the popular thing to do. And you know, we can learn something from Paul, because there are certain situations we ought not abide. There are some times when we must stand up for right and righteousness. God calls us to tell the truth. Jesus said you should know the truth and truth will set you free. But Paul does not just speak the truth. Because you know how it is—we don't really want to know the truth. Most often, the truth is difficult for us to bear. And we can be so nasty when we tell the truth. And so, Paul instructs us to speak the truth in love. It's hard enough to hear the truth. But we sure ain't gonna hear it from somebody who does not mean us any good. So, Paul speaks the truth in love. True love.

Second, Paul acts a "fool," since that seems to be the only thing the Corinthians understand, the only thing that they can relate to. He has tried being nice to them. He has tried reasoning with them. He has tried urging and compelling them. He has tried teaching them. He has tried setting an example for them. And they still didn't get it. But what I love about Paul is even in his acting a fool, he does not compromise his faith.

You know, as I said earlier, I'm a young woman pastor. Many believe that I can preach. Many believe that I can visit the sick, bury the dead, and comfort the bereaved. But few are convinced that I can pastor. You know how we are. It's clear that I've been to Mount Holyoke, that I've been to Union, that I'm educated—that's clear. Still some people try me. So every now and then, I have to remind folks that I'm from the west side of Detroit, and I know how to get ignorant, if need be. 'Cause you know how you have to get ignorant sometimes. You try to be nice to some people and they won't let you be nice.

That's what Paul does with the Corinthian church because the situation in Corinth calls for strong measures. The church was tolerating all kinds of foolishness and abuse. They were just degenerated. And Paul says in the eleventh chapter and the nineteenth verse—he's being a little facetious when he says—"For you gladly put up with fools, being wise yourselves. For you put up with it when someone makes slaves of you, or preys upon you, or takes advantage of you, or puts on airs, or even slaps you in the face." They put up with that and Paul declares that he is not willing to tolerate it any longer. He will not look the other way any longer. Why? Because he does not love them? No! *Because he does!* In contrast with those cruel and selfish so-called apostles, who talk a good game and appear to have it all together. That sound familiar?

So I ask this evening: Who do you relate to? Are you like Paul? Or are you like the Corinthians? We need true love. For love is vital and necessary, but it's not always easy to recognize. Because it doesn't always look like, and perform like, we think it ought to. This is often the case in relationships. Sisters—I'm a womanist, but I believe in speaking the truth in love—there are times when we are our own worst enemy, because we don't want anybody really who's going to be decent to us. Somehow, we get the misguided impression that if somebody's good to us, they don't really love us. If they're not causing us all kinds of heartache and pain, taking our money, humiliating us in public with all their other women, going upside our head, they don't really love us. And then that nice dutiful brother, who might seem a little nerdy and whose suits aren't always color-coordinated, but who respects us and would do anything for us, we kick him to the curb! And brothers—y'all ain't gonna escape this evening—a woman can't be a good woman, a nice and a sweet woman, or you walk all over her. So in order to get treated right, a woman's got to be a witch with a "B" right in front of it, cussin' and fussin' and raisin' all kind of sand, and then you're in love!

And you know, it's like that in churches. Isn't it astonishing that the pastors who act the worst are invited to preach in eight hundred and eleven revivals a year? They don't visit the sick, don't do funerals, don't see about the old people, don't counsel, get up every Sunday, browbeating and fussin' at their folk, drivin' the biggest Mercedes, wearing Hugo Boss suits, and getting a month-long anniversary celebration for doing nothing! It's so easy to be misled, because everything that looks good, and everything that sounds good to us, is not necessarily good for us. And some things that are good for us may not feel good initially. That's why there is such a thing as delayed gratification.

Ultimately, it's an issue of confidence and esteem, because you know what? Folks will not treat us better until we're convinced that we deserve better. We will not be loved the way we deserve to be loved until we love ourselves. And so we won't be treated better, or we won't be able to accept it when folks do treat us better, until we're convinced that we deserve better. There comes a point when we say, "I can do bad by myself. I don't need no help to do bad. I can be miserable by myself. I don't need anybody to make me miserable. I can be lonely and pitiful by myself. Why do I need to be lonely and pitiful with you?"

It is so easy to be worn down by assaults on our humanity. It is so easy to internalize the negative characterizations that we begin to think that we have no choice other than to endure mistreatment and even abuse. Yet, we do not have to be victims. We can make a conscious decision to stand up for our best interests. We can turn away from anything and anyone that is demeaning and outside our best interests. We can insist on being treated with dignity and respect, especially by those who profess to love us.

There comes a point when we must wake up and realize and recognize that we are God's children. We are God's people. And God did not make us to take abuse. God did not put us here to be mistreated. Jesus said, "I came that you would have life, and life abundantly. My love will satisfy you! Drugs and alcohol won't help you!" When we've tried everything, and everything has failed, we need to try Jesus!

True love affirms and supports our humanity. Recognizing true love requires discernment. Receiving true love takes confidence. Demonstrating true love demands faith. Christ is at the core of true love. God is the source of true love. Everyone desires true love. We all need true love. God's love in Christ is true love. Jesus proclaims, "I want to be burden-bearer, and a heavy load-sharer, a bridge over troubled water, a doctor in a sick room, a lawyer in a courtroom, bread when you're hungry, bread of Heaven — bread of Heaven feed us till we want no more — water when we're thirsty, a rock in a weary land, a shelter in a time of storm, a friend who will never forsake you, and a way out of no way!"

As I take my seat, I take the words of the hymnist, and I relate it to my own experience. When he said, "I was sinking deep in sin far from the peaceful shore, very deeply stained within, sinking to rise no more, but the master of the sea heard my despairing cry, from the waters, lifted me, now safe am I. Love lifted me, love lifted me when nothing else could help, love lifted me."

From Paternalism to Partnership
John Richard Foulkes, Sr.

By reference to Paul's letter to Philemon, this sermon asks us to contemplate whether we build our relationships based on paternalism or as a partnership based on unconditional love.

PHILEMON 1–22

THE WITNESSING OF a marriage ceremony always gives opportunity for reflection upon the intimate relationships between human beings. This service of establishing the covenant of the most intimate relationship experienced by humans, coupled with the growing epidemic divorce rate and the genocide of the African-American family, forces us to struggle with the issue of intimacy and egocentrism. Intimacy binds one's sense of self with another. Egocentrism finds one's sense of self within oneself.

Analysis of Jesus' identification of the greatest commandment in Matthew 22:36–40 supports the current therapeutic focus on self-love, enabling love of others and God. The excess of self-love noted in the "I wills" of Isaiah 14:12–15 identifies the evil that can be present in excessive egocentrism. Reflection on the temptation narrative in Matthew 4 heightens this stress, when it is realized that the basis for the temptations was the exaltation of self-will above partnership with God.

If an ambiguous relationship exists between healthy self-love and love of the other, there is a critical need for clarity about the boundaries of that ambiguity. In this age of cultural self-definition and struggle for holistic pluralistic community, the egocentric/intimacy argument takes on heightened importance. The question becomes, "Do we have, as our basic motive, *paternalism/maternalism or partnership*, as we seek relationships with others?"

The most explicit instruction that I am aware of in the Word of God on this issue is that found in Paul's letter to Philemon. Let's look closely at that instruction.

The letter opens with the image of a runaway slave, Onesimus, standing at the door of his slave owner, Philemon, with a letter from Paul in his hand. First-century law identified a slave as property and allowed the slave owner to treat that property any way that the slave owner wanted to. The slave owner could kill the slave at will without any criticism or question by the larger society.

Onesimus had not only run away from Philemon but had "wronged"[1] Philemon and was considered "useless" to him. Death would have been expected. The only thing that separated Onesimus from this sudden unquestioned death was the letter that he held in his hand.

Onesimus stood in this perilous position out of an understanding of a new relationship with his slave owner. Philemon was a Christian who had been brought to faith in Jesus Christ through the witness of the apostle Paul—Philemon owed Paul "even [his] own self." Philemon had become a "coworker" with Paul, had a "church" in his own house, and had become known throughout the region for his "love for all the saints and [his] faith toward the Lord Jesus."

This special relationship between Paul and Philemon placed Paul in a position of authority as Philemon's mentor. As his mentor, Paul was responsible for enabling/empowering Philemon. Paul could have based his mentoring on a system of wise, benevolent paternalism. Paul could have mentored Philemon based on what he had done for Philemon—"I am bold enough in Christ to command you to do your duty." Paul could have made a demand as: Philemon's agent of redemption from the God-limited existence; the mentoring/instructor of the faith; the counselor that enabled leadership of the church in Philemon's home; cosigner of the notoriety that Philemon was experiencing. Paul, however, chose a higher motivation for the partnership—"I would rather appeal to you on the basis of love."

African-American congregations initially began in the Christian Church (Disciples of Christ) at the close of the Civil War through either missionary activity by Anglo-Americans or as a result of separation of African Americans from previously integrated congregations. That same motivation of liberating into self-

---

[1]Philemon 18.

determined yet segregated existence led to the establishment of African-American educational institutions and even a partnership between those educational institutions and the newly established congregations for the education of ministers to lead those congregations and to start new ones.

Dynamics that are relatively young in the cultural development of African Americans have called for a change of self-understanding from that of being "objects of mission" to "partners in the mission." That shifting dynamic forces the agent of the missionary enterprise to consider, just as Paul had to consider in his relationship with Philemon: Do we predicate our future relationship on the paternalistic enablement of the past or "on the basis of love"?

Onesimus, aware of the new relationship that he had with Philemon and Paul's advocacy based on love, holds his physical life in the message of the letter that he holds in his hand. Verses 10 through 12 of the letter make it very obvious that Paul loved Onesimus: "I am appealing to you for my child, Onesimus, whose father I have become during my imprisonment. Formerly he was useless to you, but now he is indeed useful both to you and to me. I am sending him, that is, my own heart, back to you."

Paul refers to Onesimus as "my child," "my own heart," one "I wanted to keep" but, "I am sending him . . . to you." In his commitment of the giving of what he loved to enable a greater partnership "on the basis of love," Paul must have had a glimpse of the divine love that enabled God to give God's self for humankind that was still in the midst of rebellion against God.

For God so loved the world that he gave his only begotten Son, so that everyone who believes in him may not perish but may have eternal life.   JOHN 3:16

But God proves his love for us in that while we still were sinners Christ died for us.   ROMANS 5:8

God gave his only begotten Son to die for our sins to enable a new partnership—a partnership based on true, honest, uncompromising love for one another

It is easy to love someone who is "right" by one's own standards. It takes a whole different kind of love, partnership love, to love one who is radically different from the perceived "right."

As Onesimus stood at Philemon's door with the letter in his hand, he must have considered the reason that Paul had sent him back to Philemon. Paul must have met Onesimus as an inconspicuous person on a Roman street over one hundred miles from Philemon's house. After having established a relationship with Onesimus, having been an instrument of bringing him to faith in Christ Jesus and having experienced his care, he could have told him to keep on running. Onesimus knew that Paul had introduced him to a new freedom—a freedom in Jesus Christ. This new freedom elevated Onesimus above his social/economic status and gave him a new basis for the relationship. "On the basis of love," Philemon was no longer his slave master, but his brother in Christ.

Persons of African descent in America know all too well the dehumanization of the marginalized position fostered upon them by the majority American culture. Christian faith, which was developed by and sustains this African-American culture, is so precious to African Americans that there is great reluctance to seriously share it or allow it to become vulnerable in the majority American culture. Paul's counsel to marginalized African Americans is the same as was given to Onesimus: "I am sending him . . . back to you . . . No longer as a slave but more than a slave, a beloved brother." We can't really be free until we go back into the "garbage" and proclaim our freedom in spite of it.

When Paul and Onesimus came to this basic understanding of liberation in spite of the "garbage," some great things began to happen. Paul's love for Onesimus led him to intercede for Onesimus. It was love that made Paul stand with Onesimus, who was obviously "one of the least of these" (Matthew 25:40) and, on the basis of societal norms, wrong. Intercession may occur for many different reasons but only an intercession "on the basis of love" enables a substitution of the intercessor on behalf of the one being interceded for. Listen to the language that Paul uses:

So if you consider me your partner, welcome him as you would welcome me. If he has wronged you in any way, or owes you anything, charge that to my account.

PHILEMON 17–18

Paul tells Philemon that he wants him to receive Onesimus as if he were Paul. That slave standing in front of you, Philemon, that person that ran away from you, Philemon; that person that wronged you, Philemon; that person that you could legally kill, Philemon; receive him as if he were me and if he owes you anything, put it on my account. If you need to have the money back, I will repay it. If he is in trouble, I will stand for him.

God sent forth God's son into the world that he might stand in our place for sin's sake. For our sake he made him to be sin who knew no sin, so that in him we might become the righteousness of God.   2 CORINTHIANS 5:21

Then Jesus said, "Father, forgive them; for they do not know what they are doing." And they cast lots to divide his clothing.   LUKE 23:34

Jesus said, in effect, I have loved them and interceded for them to the extent that I have given the best that I have—I have substituted myself for them. They can now stand with each other, substituting themselves for each other. They can now be truly liberated and liberating people.

The implications of the intercession through substitution is that we are going to have to take those cantankerous, no-Christian-living, no-Christian-talking folk—you know, those folk that meet in board meetings once a month, those folk that won't do right no matter what you do, those folk that you wonder if they ever even heard about the word "Christian," those thorns in your flesh, those folk that wouldn't say anything good about you if you paid them—you are going to have to take those folk, substitute yourself in their situation and in the midst of the garbage that they are pouring out toward you, substitute love.

You may not be able to let them know that you are doing it. You may even find that if they find out that you are trying to love them, they may do something else to aggravate that attempt to love. But Christ's substitution for you compels you to love them anyhow.

Intercession brought substitution and that substitution brought about restoration. "Perhaps this is the reason he was separated from you for a while, so that you might have him back forever" (verse 15). The psalmist wrote:

> I waited patiently for the Lord; he inclined to me and heard my cry. He drew me up from the desolate pit, out of the miry bog, and set my feet upon a rock, making my steps secure. He put a new song in my mouth, a song of praise to our God. Many will see and fear, and put their trust in the Lord.
>
> PSALM 40:1–3

Praise be unto God for the substitution. The restoration takes place because of the substitution. If you have been present with others in the midst of their garbage, you can be an agent for lifting them out of that garbage. You can move them from their stumbling and ever falling deeper into the garbage to being placed on a solid rock on which they can stand. Have you ever tried to get a firm footing on mud? If so, you know that it is not only impossible but that all of your energy is drained even as you try to stand. The Jesus that rescued us from the miry clay gives us a ministry of rescuing others.

> From now on, therefore, we regard no one from a human point of view; even though we once knew Christ from a human point of view, we know him no longer in that way. So if anyone is in Christ, there is a new creation: everything old has passed away; see, everything has become new! All this is from God, who reconciled us to himself through Christ, and has given us the ministry of reconciliation; that is, in Christ God was reconciling the world to himself, not counting their trespasses against them, and entrusting the message of reconciliation to us.
>
> 2 CORINTHIANS 5:16–19

We are going to have to reach down into some miry clay pits, pull out some people, set them on some solid places, and tell them to stand there. Substitution enabled elevation:

> Perhaps this is the reason he was separated from you for a while, so that you might have him back forever, no longer as a slave, but more than a slave, a beloved brother—especially to me but how much more to you, both in the flesh and in the Lord. PHILEMON 15–16

Intercession "on the basis of love" grows out of the sharing of one's own journey and the desire for another to have that same experience of liberation. The writer of 1 John put it this way: "We declare to you what we have seen and heard so that you also may have fellowship with us; and truly our fellowship is with the Father and with his Son Jesus Christ (I John 1:3).

Reflect on the struggles that have taken place in your life and the pits that you have found yourself struggling in. Then think about how good it has been to get all cleaned up. You don't feel like the same person.

You have reached down and taken yourself out of the mud experience. Jesus took you out of the spiritual mud of your life and placed your foot on a solid rock. Do you know of sisters or brothers who are still in the mud pits? If so, do you feel comfortable standing on a solid rock while your sister or brother is still in the mud pit?

Articles that I read speak of the increased progress of the African-American middle class. Those same articles speak of the recent development of an African-American "underclass"—persons who are so deeply entrenched in poverty and oppression that they have no hope of ever being liberated.

Some of us have been elevated. We drive pretty cars, live in nice homes, wear nice suits and dresses, have a few shirts in the drawer. We generally feel good about ourselves and often forget about our brothers and sisters that have been pushed so far down that they have become hopeless.

The strange thing is that if those who think they have arrived would compare the most successful African-American-owned business with the businesses listed on the Fortune 500 list, we would realize that we have not even begun to be in the same ballpark. Do we possibly feel good because we look good only because there is someone else who doesn't look as good?

Substitution brought about elevation. "He put a new song in my mouth, a song of praise to our God." I've got something to talk about. I can praise God, not because everything is going well for me but because, in the midst of my garbage, I've moved from being a victim to being a nonvictim. Although I might stand all dirty and filthy, the filth I stand in does not have to be who I am.

Paul said to Philemon, "Listen, Phil, there was a slave that ran away; there's a brother coming back. I could demand some things from you because I am in a parental relationship with you. I don't want to ask as a parent. I want to function with you as a partner. I am not interested in paternalism anymore, Philemon. I am interested in partnership."

African-American members of the Christian Church, we have to let go of paternalism and struggle for partnership. He may have left as a servant, but Phil, Oney is coming back as a brother!!

There is no longer Jew or Greek, there is no longer slave or free, there is no longer male and female; for all of you are one in Christ Jesus.   GALATIANS 3:28

A MOTHER AT THE CROSS
C. L. Franklin

We are reminded in this powerfully cadent Mother's Day sermon that we must recognize and appreciate maternal love as exhibited by Christ's mother, Mary.

JOHN 19:25–27

I WANT TO talk with you this evening from a passage found in the Book of St. John, the nineteenth chapter, the twenty-fifth through the twenty-seventh verse. "Now there stood by the cross of Jesus his mother, and his mother's sister, Mary the wife of Cleophas, and Mary Magdalene. When Jesus therefore saw his mother, and the disciple standing by, whom he loved, he said unto his mother, Woman, behold thy son! Then said he to the disciple, Behold thy mother! And from that hour the disciple took her unto his own home."

Now I want to talk about a mother at the cross. I think the thing that makes us identify ourselves with Jesus is his humanness. I thank God that he didn't make him without the tendency of temptation. I thank God that the Lord made him in such a way that he got hungry, he got tired, he got sleepy, he got lonely. He wept, cried like you cry sometimes.

In this instance he did something very characteristic of himself, that under the spell of excruciating pain, in an hour when he felt like even God had forsaken him, when darkness was not only upon him physically but darkness was upon him mentally and spiritually—we have those hours sometimes with us, for in our lives some rain falls, some winds blow, some storms arise—but characteristic, characteristic of him because under those unusual circumstances he thought about others: He thought about his mother.

Now his mother had been with him from birth. She was at the cradle, she was in the home, she was in and out of the carpenter's shop. She walked backwards and forward to Jerusalem along with him. Those were not hard places, bad places, but the thing that makes this experience unique is that she was not only at all of these other places, she was at the cross. (I don't believe you're praying with me tonight.)

She was at the cross. Now there are some theological commentators who said that while Peter had denied him and many of the others had deserted him and Judas had betrayed him, Mary was there. Some of the commentators say that she was there because she was permitted to be there under the cultural situation, that women were not thought of as equals in anything, in responsibility or anything else. It is said that women were almost unnoticed. But this is a sad commentary.

Anytime a man has been charged with treason—hmmm? Anytime the Roman government has ruled that you are guilty of treason, it's dangerous for anybody to be with you. (Did you hear me?) Anytime the Jewish church had decreed that he was a heretic, an impostor, and a devil—I want to tell you, it was dangerous for Mary to be there.

You know, if you've read this Scripture with any care, the Scripture surrounding the trial and crucifixion of Jesus—the arrest, the trial, and the crucifixion, you'll notice that the charge was first a religious charge. He had blasphemed against God, according to the high priests. But the country, Judea, although the Jews had some rights, they did not have the right of capital punishment. (Did you hear me?)

And of course when they came up with that charge, Herod wouldn't deal with it. "Now you've got to get us another charge. Now whatever he's done to offend you-all here in your church, we can't deal with that. It's certainly not deserving capital punishment. If you want him put to death you got to come up with a better charge than that." And they went back and brought up treason, saying that he was working against Caesar; he was working against the state; he was inspiring and instigating a revolution against Rome. Then Caesar said, "Well now . . ." or Pilate said, "Well, I can deal with that now. If he's doing anything against the state, then we can deal with him."

Now I'm trying to say that through it all, Mary was there. His mother was there. Cecil [Franklin] talked about the qualifications of a mother this morning, and motherhood was not just something biological, but is something that one has to earn. Just because you have had a child doesn't make you a mother! Motherhood is something that one has to achieve. Well, I'm trying to tell you that Mary was a model mother. She not only brought him into this world, she taught him the traditions of his people. She saw to it that he observed all of the rites, all of the ceremonies. And here at the end, she was there. Didn't have the privilege of being at his bedside. It was worse than that. She was standing by his cross.

Say, "Well, why wasn't she scared?" Love rules out fear. Say, "Well, he has broken the law." Love doesn't care anything about breaking the law. Some folks say, "I love you when you're right, but when you're wrong I'm through with you." Then you don't love. Because if you love me, you're with me right or wrong. You're there to help me get strength if I'm wrong.

She was at his cross. Her sister was there, and then Mary Magdalene was there. Her sister, who was the mother of James and John, had come to him one day and said, "Well now, I know that you are going to follow the messianic tradition and I know you're about to get your kingdom set up and organized. I want my two sons to be closest to the throne. I want James on one side. I want John on the other. Don't have too much time to worry about other folks' children; I'm talking about mine." Jesus pointed out to her the selfishness of her ambition but it didn't crush her, for she was working for her own children, she was functioning as a mother. (You don't hear me tonight. Listen if you please.)

I believe it was Rudyard Kipling who said,

If I were hanged from the highest hill,
　Mother, o mother of mine,
I know whose love would follow me still,
　Mother, o mother of mine.
If I were damned—or drowned, rather, in the deepest sea,
　Mother, o mother of mine,
I know whose love would come down to me,
　Mother, o mother of mine.
If I were damned of body and soul,

> Mother, o mother of mine,
> I know whose prayers would make me whole,
> Mother of mine, o mother of mine.

She was at the cross. I tell you, if one is in the deepest sea, she's there or her prayers are there. If you're damned body and soul her love and prayers will make you whole.

So Jesus said, "Woman," which was not derogatory, considering it within the framework of his culture. It was not disrespectful. He said, "Woman, behold your son." Said, "Now I know I'm about to leave here. I'm hanging from a tree. And my weight is tearing the flesh in my hands. But I want to see that you have a home before I leave here. I want you to have somewhere to go. Now I've got some brothers but I can't leave you with my burdens because they don't believe in me." (I wish I had somebody here to pray.) "I want to leave you with somebody who believes that God has wrought a miracle in my life." (You don't hear me today.)

That was one of the things he said from the cross. Another one—I said he was concerned about others—another one was, "Father, forgive them, for they know not what they do." And then, "Verily I say unto thee, today thou shalt be with me in Paradise." And then, "Father, into thine hands I commend my spirit." These were things that he said while he was dying.

Somebody said he stopped dying long enough to run revival and take one of the thieves along with him. (You don't hear me.) Stopped dying and prayed for them, and said, "This day you'll be with me in Paradise." And then he said, right after he appointed Mary a home, "I thirst. I've been out here since noon, hanging on this tree. I've been out here under unusual tropical sun. I've been losing blood since last night. But I wanted to get at least one of the thieves straight. And then I wanted to pray for everybody who's doing things against themselves and others. I wanted to pray for them before it's over. And then I want to commit and commend my spirit to God." And certainly he did. And when he said that, he dropped his head, and said, "It's finished. The battle is over. The task has been completed. The work has been done. To this end was I born.

And

    for this cause
      came I
      into the world.

And

    it's finished now.

O Lord.

    I don't need
      anybody
      to commit me.
    I don't need
      anybody
      to read the burial ceremony.

Well

    I'm going to say it
      myself.

Yes I am.

    Into your hands
      I commend my spirit.

O Lord."
And

    I remember reading
      a story a long time ago
      that dealt with
    mother's eternal love.
    It is said
      that her son
      was in jail,
    and he was in there
      because he had been condemned
      to die.

O Lord.

    They were going to put a rope
      around his neck

and

    the hangman
    was going to remove
    the plank on which he was standing.

O Lord.

And
they
had tried
    and failed
    time and again
    to get him a reprieve.

O Lord.

And every time
    they failed.

O Lord.

The mother
thought about an old
    tradition
    that went on and obtained
    in that country:
Before they hanged
anybody
    they had to ring the bell.

O Lord.

And early that morning
    she got up
and went down
    to the courthouse
    where
    the gallows had been situated.

O Lord.

She climbed up
in the belfry
    about an hour
    before time.

O Lord.

And
then the hangman
and his crowd
    came marching out.

And

    she was up in the belfry

holding on
   to the bell clapper.
O Lord.

They got the rope
   in their hands.
They pulled down
   but there was no sound.
And as they pulled the bell,
the bell swung over
   from one side to another.
O Lord.

She fell
against the iron wall
   of that big bell.
O Lord.
She was bruised,
she was bleeding,
but she held on
   to the bell clapper,
oh yes she did.
Yes.
And after a while
   they gave up.
After a while
they said, "Since the bell won't ring,
   we can't execute him."
O Lord.

By that time
she fell down
   upon the ground
   under the bell clapper
with blood
running from her nose,
from her eyes
   and from her shoulders.
O Lord.

She said, "Well, son,

I know you meant good.
You are my child.
Go on.
Don't worry.
Don't worry
about me.
I'm all right."
O Lord.
Did you know
that Jesus,
　Jesus
held the bell clapper
of time and eternity
　in his hands?
Oh well,
ohh,
yes!

LOVE OF SELF
Howard Thurman

In this thoughtful sermon, we are challenged to grapple with our own individuality and the godliness within each of us. We are encouraged to love our ever-evolving selves and to reject negative and destructive self-images which deny God's love and power.

Meditation

Strong Son of God. Immortal Love . . .
Who we that have not seen thy face,
By faith and faith alone embrace.
Believing where we cannot prove,
Our little systems have their day, they have their day,
and cease to be.
They are but broken lights of thee.
But thou, O Lord, art more than they.
Our father,
Amen.

I WANT TO begin by reading two things. First is a parable. And it is called "The Animal School." And I want you to hold in mind without trying to decide what on earth do I mean by reading it to you until after we are through, and maybe tomorrow or the next day. Or perhaps never will you understand, but that does not mean that it is not understood.

Once upon a time the animals decided they must do something heroic to meet the problems of the new world. So they organized a school. They adopted an activity curriculum consisting of running, climbing, swimming, and flying. And to make it easy to administer, all of the animals had to take all of the subjects. The duck was excellent in swimming—better, in fact, than his instructor—and made passing grades in flying, but was very poor in running. Since he was slow in running, he had to stay after school and drop swimming to practice running. This was kept up until his feet were badly worn and he was only average, at last, in swimming. But average was acceptable in that school so nobody worried about that, except the duck.

The rabbit started at the top of the class in running, but had a nervous breakdown because of so much make-up work in swimming.

The squirrel was excellent in climbing until he developed frustration in the flying class, where his teacher made him start from the ground up instead of from the treetop down. He also developed charley horses from overexertion and got a C in climbing and a D in running.

The eagle was a problem child and was disciplined severely in the climbing class, for even though he beat all the others to the top of the tree he insisted in using his own way to get up there. At the end of the year, an abnormal eel that could swim exceedingly well and also run, climb, and fly a little had the highest average and was valedictorian. Prairie dogs stayed out of school and fought the tax levy because the administration would not add digging and burrowing to the curriculum. They apprenticed their child to a badger and later joined the groundhog and gophers to start a successful private school.

This is a quotation:

"In a man's hotel room, he picked up a card and the card said, 'Need spiritual vitamins? If so, call. Dial A-DEVOTION Phone 7430424. When out of town call 211-4204730424. If it is busy call 2114204730425.' "

"He did not need spiritual vitamins.

"He went to church. At the outside door he passed under a closed-circuit camera. At the inner sanctuary doors, he took a ticket extended to him by the click of a machine. The ticket said, 'Our observer on T notes that you are a newcomer. We have recorded your picture for our files. You are assigned number 40697-7042b-308110. Your IBM card will be ready at coffee fellowship time this noon. Sit in pew 4C. At offering time you will be handed a three-year pledge card, 156 blank checks, 156 stamped envelopes so that you can have the warm sense of participation even when you are out of town.'

"At the Sunday evening rally he was attendant number 18423, decision number 424. On Tuesday he received a notice saying one of the cards had crumpled and he was asked to come to church on Thursday evening to straighten it out.

"Thursday evening. Went to straighten it out. Found the trouble. Found that the trouble often happens that IBM cards get bent when another card is inserted with it in the file. A person told *me* so, in person. Friday, *I* took some sort of extra card and inserted it in the file so that I would have to go every Thursday and perchance meet a person."

Growing in Love. Apostle Paul says, "My prayer to God is that your love may grow more and more rich in knowledge and in all manner of insight that you may have a sense, a feel for what is vital. That you may be transparent and of no harm to anyone in view of the day of Christ. Your life covered with that harvest of righteousness that Jesus produces to the praise and to the glory of God. My prayer to God is that you may grow more and more rich in knowledge. And in all manner of insight, growing in love. In love of myself."

One of the great and critical problems of our time is that it is very difficult to find ourselves, for a person to find himself, to know where he is, who he is, what is he. And we think of love — when we think of it — in terms of feelings, thoughts, caring, all the words that you might use, for a not-self, for some other person, and we have so rearranged our inner sense of values that even we are loath to admit that we should love ourselves.

Now, I cannot love myself if I am anonymous to myself. If I have no idea about who I am, I cannot get close enough to me to love me. I spend my time trying to find me in the midst of the wide range of images of me that have been projected into me from my earliest childhood, by those who cared for me, who loved me, and who nurtured me. So that it is a very difficult and perilous route to locate me, to separate me from the self-images of me that are projected upon me from the time I am a baby. Images that reflect the love — sometimes. The images that reflect the self-rejection on the part of those whose responsibility it is to care for and nurture me. The image reflected upon me by my environment, so that wherever I look, I see thrown on the screen of my awareness a picture of me which, the assumption is, reflects not what is in the mind of the persons who cast the image before me, but a reflection of what I think I am.

So that before I can get to whatever may be "myself" facts, I've got to work through all of these images. I am my mother's boy. I am my father's son. I am my sister's brother. I am my aunt's nephew. But, WHO ON EARTH AM I? WHO AM I? How may I draw a bead on me?

I think of myself always in relative terms, so that I spent the early days of my life fitting into a whole series of images. And I don't know who I am, who I am. One day I came into the house, in the early days of the church in San Francisco, and I was full of all the aroma of frustration and it went up the stairs ahead of me and when I came into the room I said something to my daughter and I referred to her as my daughter. Of course she is her mother's daughter and it is against that lineage that she addressed me. She said, "Nobody has ever seen a daughter. I'm not a daughter. I'm Ann. And thirteen years old. . . ." And so and so. She gave me the catalogue. And up to that time, I was sure that of course I wasn't the best father in the world, but I was number two. Without being aware of it, I had thought of her in the abstract. And what she needed from me was to think of her in particular, in the concrete.

Love myself. How can I find me?

Now, let's take two or three steps. First, I must accept my fact. Now think with me a little about this. I MUST ACCEPT MY FACT. And perhaps the emotionally healthy person is one who is able to maintain a tension between his or herself—fact—and one's self-image. Every time you make a new discovery about you, that you embrace as something that is genuinely and authentically a part of you, every time you do this, then the image that you had of yourself before you were aware of this fact has to be reordered and rearranged. For instance, suppose all of your life you had been healthy. You knew what sickness was vicariously. So that the self-image that you have is of a robust, healthy human being. Then suppose your health fails or you become a cripple. Now, this is a new self-fact. My problem is to introduce this new fact about me into my self-image of me. The degree to which I am able to do that allows me to be whole, have a sense of wholeness. But, if I am unable to do it, then this fact that I cannot introduce into my own self-image, I must drag it around on the outside of me. And of course, sometimes, it is out of this that invalids are made.

I can't find a way to introduce this new discovery about myself, a new fact, into the image I had of myself before I knew this. To love one's self against this background is to deal with oneself at a center. And this is the heart of what I want to say. Now let me say it again: to deal with myself at a point in myself that is not limited by my faults and my virtues. This is why it is so important that I grow in understanding of myself, because there is so much more to me than what I am doing at any time. There is so much more to me than I can ever express, so that whatever I do as I look at it from within this center, I know that this thing that I have done does not quite represent what I was trying to do.

So, I must have tomorrow. I must have another day, for perhaps if I can live long enough, I can locate the deeds at my center, and that's why I never give myself up. I may give you up. But I cling to myself with persistence and abiding enthusiasm, for whatever may be the reading from out there, I see what no one else out there can see. I am standing on the inside.

Now that's the "love yourself" that's very different from selfishness. It's very different from an ego trip and all these other nice words we use. But it is recognizing that no one like me has ever existed in all the ages, all the generations. No one, no one, but me is me. That's better a thing than "I." Feels better. No face like mine has ever been born. Everything in existence stands aside to salute the first coming of man in you, you, you, me. And therefore, I dare not abuse me.

This body of mine is the only dwelling place of my mind and my spirit. I have no other dwelling place. And if I so disown my organism because I am ashamed of it or because it's broken or because it is ugly or unsightly, there is no other place for me. So with all my limitations, with all my inadequacies, with all the things about me that are unsightly and unseemly, this is it. And anyone who wishes to destroy me, all he has to do is to make me hate me. So that I'm ashamed of me and I'm a wanderer in the vast spaces of an empty universe. No home, nowhere.

So when I love myself, I honor myself. I place a crown over my head that all of my years I'm trying to grow tall enough to wear. I don't excuse myself, I don't apologize for me. As Abraham Lincoln said: "God could have made me a better-looking man, but he didn't. So I have to do the best I can with what I have." And if anything is internalized by me from doctrine, dogma, philosophy, propaganda—anything that makes me say about me: I don't count—this is violence against God. So to apply the great injunction of the apostle, my prayer to God is that your love of yourself will grow more and more in knowledge and understanding, that you may have a sense of what is vital, that you may be transformed and of no harm to yourself, your life covered with all of the graces and the beauty that caused God to rejoice when he gave you your life.

And my prayer is that God will not be driven to repentance because he brought me into the world.

AUTHOR BIOGRAPHIES

REV. DR. MARTIN LUTHER KING, JR. (1929–1968)

Dr. Martin Luther King, Jr., is widely recognized as one of the greatest orators in American history and one of our nation's finest preachers and theologians. A graduate of Morehouse College and Crozer Theological Seminary, Dr. King earned his doctorate at Boston University School of Theology in June 1955. Beginning with a successful boycott against the Montgomery, Alabama, public bus system, Dr. King was the most prominent leader of America's civil rights movement through his adherence to nonviolent protest and civil disobedience. The recipient of many awards, Dr. King received the Nobel Prize for Peace in 1964. He was assassinated in April 1968 at the age of thirty-nine. Dr. King's prophetic words both influenced and inspired clergy and parishioners all over the world and helped lead the United States through its most turbulent times of social unrest.

FLOYD H. FLAKE

In his role as pastor of the Allen A.M.E. Church, Jamaica, New York, since 1976, the Rev. Flake has witnessed the explosive growth of the church from a congregation of 1,400 to one of more than 8,000 worshipers. In 1986, he was elected to the House of Representatives, where he has advocated an effort to bring more focus and greater understanding of America's urban agenda to the Congress. A graduate of Wilberforce University, Rev. Flake also holds a doctorate of ministry from the United Theological Seminary in Dayton, Ohio.

JEREMIAH A. WRIGHT, JR.

Dr. Wright is senior pastor of the five thousand member Trinity United Church of Christ in Chicago, Illinois's largest congregation in that denomination. He holds degrees from Virginia Union University, Howard University, the University of Chicago Divinity School, and the United Theological Seminary. In addition to being a renowned preacher, Dr. Wright is a professor, community leader, and host of his own radio program. He is the author of *What Makes You So Strong? Sermons of Joy and Strength.*

TOINETTE M. EUGENE

Dr. Eugene is currently the associate professor of Christian social ethics at the Garrett-Evangelical Theological Seminary in Evanston, Illinois. She received her

B.A. in English literature at the University of San Francisco, and her M.A. in theology and education and Ph.D. in religion and society from the Graduate Theological Union in Berkeley, California. Dr. Eugene is a member of the American Academy of Religion, the Society of Christian Ethics, the Journal of Moral Education, and the Society for the Study of Black Religion, among others. Her writings on theology and women's issues have appeared in numerous journals and books.

REGINALD T. JACKSON

Reverend Jackson is pastor of St. Matthew's A.M.E. Church in Orange, New Jersey. A native of Dover, Delaware, he is a graduate of Delaware State College and the Interdenominational Theological Center in Atlanta. Rev. Jackson is a member of the Board of Education in the city of Orange, a member of the Governing Board of the New Jersey Council of Churches, and political action chairman and executive director of the Newark–North Jersey Committee of Black Churchmen. He is a widely respected leader on social, humanitarian, and spiritual issues throughout the state of New Jersey and nationally.

FELECIA YVONNE THOMAS

Reverend Thomas is the first woman pastor of the historic First Baptist Church in Princeton, New Jersey. A graduate of Mount Holyoke College and Union Theological Seminary, she is the recipient of numerous awards and honors, including the Benjamin E. Mays Fellowship and the Maxwell Fellowship. She has served as convener of the Alliance of African-American Women in Ministry of the American Baptist Churches, as a member of the editorial board of *The Living Pulpit,* and a trustee for the New Jersey Convention of Progressive Baptists. In 1993, she was cited by the *New York Daily News* as one of New York City's best preachers.

JOHN RICHARD FOULKES, SR.

Reverend Foulkes is the deputy general minister, vice president for inclusive ministries, and administrative secretary of the National Convocation for the Christian Church (Disciples of Christ). He formerly pastored Parkway Gardens Christian Church in Chicago. Rev. Foulkes holds degrees from Chicago State University and McCormick Theological Seminary.

C. L. (CLARENCE LAVAUGHN) FRANKLIN (1915–1984)

Reverend C. L. Franklin was born in a rural Mississippi community in 1915. It was at St. Peter's Rock Baptist Church in Mississippi that he was baptized and ordained to preach. Rev. Franklin studied at LeMoyne College in Memphis and the University of Buffalo. He became prominent after assuming the pastorship of New Bethel Church in Detroit. With a congregation numbering more than ten thousand in the late 1950s, Rev. Franklin reached thousands of additional worshipers throughout the country with his radio broadcasts, recordings, and preaching tours. Rev. Franklin is often remembered as a prophet who masterfully combined soul and science in his inspirational words and is frequently cited for his "whooping" preaching style, which is today prevalent among African-American clergy.

HOWARD THURMAN (1900–1981)

Poet, mystic, philosopher, and theologian, Howard Thurman was the foremost African-American spiritualist of his time. When he died in 1981, Dr. Thurman was dean emeritus of Marsh Chapel, Boston University, and chairman of the board of trustees of the Howard Thurman Educational Trust in San Francisco. An ordained Baptist minister, Dr. Thurman also served as dean of Rankin Chapel, Howard University, professor at Howard University School of Religion; and director of religious life at Morehouse and Spelman colleges in Atlanta. He was founder of the Church for the Fellowship of All Peoples in San Francisco, the first interracial, interdenominational church in the United States, and also served as honorary canon of the Cathedral of Saint John the Divine in New York City. Dr. Thurman authored more than twenty books, including *Meditations of the Heart, Jesus and the Disinherited,* and *The Inward Journey.*

About the Editors

RHINOLD PONDER

Rhinold Ponder, an attorney and literary agent, has taught African-American literature, politics, and law at Rutgers University, City University of New York (CUNY), and St. Peter's College in New Jersey, where he was the director of the black studies program. He has edited numerous publications, including the *NYU Review of Law and Social Change*, and his social commentary has appeared in the *New York Times*, *Miami Herald*, and the *City Sun*. A graduate of Princeton University, he achieved his J.D. at New York University Law School and his M.A. in journalism and M.S. in African-American studies from Boston University.

MICHELE TUCK-PONDER

Michele Tuck-Ponder is the mayor of Princeton Township, New Jersey. She has served as press secretary to Congressman Louis Stokes, special assistant to United States Senator Frank Lautenberg, assistant counsel to New Jersey Governor Jim Florio, deputy director of the New Jersey Division on Women, and assistant director of the New Jersey Division on Civil Rights. She earned a J.D. from the University of Pennsylvania Law School and a B.S. in journalism from Northwestern University. In 1990, she founded the New Jersey African-American Organ Donor Awareness Organization, and serves on a number of boards and commissions throughout the state of New Jersey.